How To Survive Y2k Chaos In The City

A Preparedness and Self-Reliance Handbook

By
Ken Eirich
Nancy Eirich

Infoage Consulting and Publishing

Dedication

This book is dedicated to our dear friend Virginia M. Macleod, without whom this book would not have been possible. We thank her for her trust and her hard work in the production of the book.

Inquiries and additional orders (*add $3.00 S & H*) should be addressed to:
Infoage Consulting and Publishing
P.O. Box 20131, Grantham Postal Outlet, St. Catharines, Ontario, Canada L2M 7W7

Disclaimer

This publication is designed to provide general information in regard to the subject matters covered. This information should be used as a general guide only and not as the absolute source of information. Statements regarding the Year 2000 Computer Crisis are, at the time presented, believed to be an accurate portrayal of facts; however, because no one can predict the future, the information provided must be accepted as opinion based on research and observation. Also, this publication is distributed with the understanding that neither the authors nor the publisher are engaged in rendering professional consultation services, legal, medical, technical or any other service. This publication should not be utilized as a substitute for seeking the advice of a professional when required. Please note: Neither the authors nor the publisher are liable or responsible to any person or entity for any loss, damage, adverse effects or consequences, caused or alleged to be caused, directly or indirectly, from the use of any of the information, suggestions, preparations or procedures in this book. Do not refer to the book if you are unwilling to assume the risk.

Canadian Cataloguing in Publication Data
Eirich, Ken, 1946 –
How to Survive Y2k Chaos in the City: A Preparedness and Self-Reliance Handbook.

Includes Index
ISBN 0-9684293-0-0

1. Survival skills 2. Survival and emergency equipment. 3. Home economics. 4. City dwellers. 5. Year 2000 date conversion (Computer systems) – Social aspects. I. Eirich, Nancy, 1952- . II. Title.
GF86.E37 1998 640'.49 C99-930035-0

Printed in Canada

Table of Contents

Y2k — A City And Urban Challenge 5
Living Without Electricity 13
Water — Is It Safe To Drink? 23
A Personalized Guide to Preparedness 33
Self-Reliance Guidelines 39
Ten Common Food-Storage Mistakes 49
Food Storage — What Are Your Choices? 51
Back to Basics Cookery 59
Campstove Cookin' 75
Substitutions and Equivalents 79
Last Minute — Low Budget Preparations 81
Keeping Your Survival Cupboard Safe 83
Preventing Food Poisoning 85
The Kitchen Gardener — Sprouting 87
Small Space Gardening 89
The City Root Cellar 99
Your Own On-Going Meat Supply 103
Barter — The New Economy 107
Index 109

City And Urban Survival Education Series

Congratulations on your purchase of the best, most practical book on city and urban survival in the marketplace.

Every suggestion in this book is achievable, practical and realistic for everyone whether you live in the city or in the country. However, you bought more than a book; you bought an on-going relationship with the authors via their Internet website. We welcome you to drop in and take advantage of our growing wealth of survival information, hints and tips that will be posted and accessible to you over the next year.

Each month a newsletter loaded with hints and tips will be posted on the site. Let us interact with you. If you have any questions on survival, drop us an e-mail. We'll research the truth and post the results.

E-mail address: mail@y2kcauses.com

http://www.y2kcauses.com

Y2k — A City And Urban Challenge

Why This Book?

Quite frankly, this book came about because certain disaster is looming just over the horizon! A disaster that will adversely affect the lives of almost everyone on earth within the same, short 24 hour period of time! A disaster that will cause critical shortages of food and water, disrupt electricity and all forms of communication, shut down the banks, and bring about massive, unprecedented levels of unemployment. It is a disaster that is certain to bring the entire world economy to its knees! It is Y2k!

After much research into the Y2k problem, we became convinced that it is a problem that the world cannot escape! We also realized that most city dwellers wouldn't know what to do when confronted by all the problems that Y2k will generate.

Since the majority of people live in the city — including ourselves — we began to look for information to help us prepare. We couldn't find anything specific to the needs of city dwellers!

Most of the information out there is to help people live off the land, but always in either a *rural* or *wilderness* setting. However, the majority of city dwellers are not equipped or capable of suddenly becoming overnight pioneers or survivalists. If caught unprepared, most city dwellers are particularly vulnerable, and will experience the greatest hardships. We city-folk, therefore, need some practical, down-to-earth information on how to become as prepared and self-reliant as we can, in our apartment, condo, townhouse or in our own home.

This is *the* foundational book in a series of books designed to help you to prepare and become self-reliant, *before* Y2k descends upon us. It is the *only* book you will need to do a fine job of survival in the city, but you may find that you would like to learn more about container gardening, sprouting, food storage, or have some specific survival recipes. This is where the other books will come in.

This is a book on preparation. You can, however, only prepare *before* the actual crisis happens. After it happens, it's too late to prepare; shortages and exorbitant prices will make survival difficult, if not impossible. Please don't put off until tomorrow what you can do today. Start right away! Time is short!

Being prepared gives you peace of mind, and ensures that you and your family will survive. That is the purpose of this book.

CITY AND URBAN
SURVIVAL EDUCATION SERIES

What is Y2k?

Y2k is technobabble for the Year 2000. It signifies the moment in time that our calendars roll over from midnight, December 31, 1999 into the year 2000. The time change in itself, however, isn't the problem. The real problem — the one that is destined to change our life — is a simple, little computer programming glitch. A glitch which is already proving itself to be the biggest technical *"foo-pah"* in recorded history!

So What Exactly is the Problem?

The roots of our problem go back to the time when computers were just being introduced some thirty to forty years ago. Unlike modern computers, these older computers were incredibly expensive and so huge that they filled entire rooms. Memory space was limited and very expensive.

To save on this precious memory, programmers entered dates with only two digits instead of four. For example, 1962 was entered as "62," instead of 1962; and 1998 would be entered as "98," instead of 1998.

This system will work well until the computer clocks roll over to the year 2000. How will the digits "00" be interpreted by most computers? Because of the programming, most computers will interpret the year 2000 as the year 1900! As a result, computer systems will either shut down or spew out incorrect data and become unreliable! Unfortunately, these outdated computer systems and programs still control almost every aspect of our modern lives, and this is why we should expect some serious problems in the near future.

Myopic Programmers?

When these computer programs were being written, this memory and cost saving procedure was applauded as brilliant. The cost savings over time easily ran into the multi-millions of dollars per megabyte of storage! So, we can't really accuse these programmers of being nearsighted.

To be fair, no programmer thought his/her program would still be in use in ten years. And, back in the '60s and '70s, this was a completely reasonable assumption. Unfortunately, it didn't happen that way! Most of those programs *(now called legacy systems, because those that developed them are either dead or retired)* are still being used today.

What's even worse, and here's the real *foo-pah,* is that nobody ever decided that it was time to change the system and incorporate a 4 digit date until the time remaining up to the year 2000 was perilously short! Then everybody went into denial and started saying, *"don't worry, they'll fix it!"*

Unfortunately, they can no longer fix it! There aren't enough programmers in the world, or time remaining to wade through the estimated 180 billion lines of code that must be screened worldwide.

The Social Security Administration in the U.S. began working on some 30 million lines of code in 1991. In June, 1996, after 5 years of work, four hundred full-time computer programmers had repaired only 6 million lines of code!

It is estimated that over 750,000 person-years will be needed to repair and test all Y2k-sensitive software! And that is for the U.S. alone! According to the Yourdons' book, *Time Bomb 2000*, the 30 most significant industrialized countries require a staggering 3.5 million person-years of effort!

To rub salt into the wound, these old programs were written in a choice of over 2500 different computer languages, many of which are now obsolete, and understood by few modern programmers! Some programmers even used silly names like the name of their pets or their favorite food to designate certain things in their program! As a result, no *"magic bullet"* solution is possible! Every single line of code must be individually corrected and tested within proper operating parameters. Do we have a problem?

Embedded Microprocessors.

These same memory/space saving tactics were incorporated in the production of an estimated 25 billion microprocessors! Every single one of these microprocessor chips has an electronic timing circuit (*a clock*) etched into the silicon chip, for timing functions. Experts believe that only a small percentage of these embedded chips are Y2k sensitive and mission critical (*failure will cause damage, process interruption, hardship or even death*)!

However, if only 0.2% of the estimated 25 billion chips are Y2k defective, that still leaves us with 50 million repair jobs! Please note that this is the LOW end of the current estimated failures! The HIGH end gives us 500,000,000 problems!

One of the main difficulties with the embedded chips is that many of them were used in places that are now almost impossible to access, places such as: satellites in orbit around the earth or microchips submerged hundreds of feet below the ocean surface in offshore oil platforms. Some chips will cost as much as 500,000 dollars each or more to replace!

In many instances, microprocessor chips were specifically designed for a project and when the project was completed, the chips were no longer produced. As a result, the entire device or sub-assembly must either be remanufactured or the offending chip will have to be redesigned and reproduced and replaced in the device.

Embedded microprocessor chips are used in almost everything. They are used in manufacturing and process control; bank vaults; every form of power generation —

including hydro, coal-fired and nuclear; water and sewage systems; oil refineries and related storage facilities; airplanes and air traffic control; radar; trains and train routing; automobiles; city traffic control and lights; banking; finance; automated teller systems; credit card services; cable systems; telephone exchanges; medical equipment; ships and satellites; and industrial process controls, just to name a few.

How many of the more than 600 communications satellites orbiting the earth will fail because of one or more embedded chips? And, what will those failures do to our vast communications network? What will these communications failures do to the North American power grid?

So Why Don't "They" Just Fix It?

Our modern world has become so complex that we have been forced to specialize in every field. As a result, few people even know about the existence of embedded systems, let alone have the ability to fix them. In addition, it can be extraordinarily difficult to assess the internal logic of the typical microprocessor — what really does it do? To look at it, it's just a black slug of plastic with a dozen or even a hundred tiny metal legs soldered into a printed circuit board or plugged into a matching socket. It's what's inside — the circuitry that is microscopically etched into the silicon — that counts! *(no pun intended)!*

Also, since testing an embedded system can damage the system or cause a malfunction, it can be an extremely lengthy, time consuming process. In addition, the testing of these microprocessor chips usually requires the entire process to be shut down — if possible — and can be very costly in lost production and manpower.

The important thing to know here is that any one of these chips can shut down an entire factory line or even put down the power grid of North America! We don't even know where all these chips are or what they control! Many were built and installed twenty or more years ago and who even knows they're there? We can't just turn the clocks ahead to find out where the offending culprits are, because most of them are independent of any type of master control. The year 2000 is almost certain to start out with a bang! A BIG one!

Why *Won't* We Make It?

There isn't any *one* reason, but many. However, starting at the top, we find both our political and industrial leaders in a chronic state of denial! Tragically, even now, many are just *evaluating* the situation — a situation which may take a decade or more to correct! We only have — as of the time of this writing — 13½ months left!

There is simply far too much to do and not enough trained personnel to do the job. Liability concerns are preventing many of the retired programmers from re-entering the arena and many of the more savvy younger programmers are already starting to run for the hills, putting the survival of their families ahead of all else. Who can blame them?

The worldwide commitment level to solving the Y2k problem has been — and still is, dismally low. *Europe* has been tinkering with the Eurodollar and has spent little time resolving more critical Y2k issues. Recent surveys show that well over 70% of *German* companies will *NOT* make it by the year 2000! *Asia, Russia* and *Japan* have been in severe economic turmoil over the past year and have done hardly anything on Y2k. *Canada, Britain, Australia,* and *France* are all hovering about 15 - 20% completed on their Y2k repairs. Most *South American* countries are far too short on financial resources and manpower to do much about Y2k!

To frustrate matters, the media calls anyone who attempts to awaken people to the truth, a doomsayer, and is presently doing little to increase awareness. This *will* change dramatically over the next year!

The Domino Effect.

Tragically, it's safe to say that almost 50% of businesses and governments around the world will *NOT* be Y2k compliant by the year 2000! We believe this to be a *conservative* estimate! Realities *after* 2000 may well prove to be much worse!

Any given corporation or government entity may themselves be 100% Y2k compliant, and yet be brought down by non-compliant suppliers. For instance, General Motors regularly deals with more than 85,000 suppliers. Each of these suppliers, in turn, depends upon other suppliers, who depend upon others, who depend...

Even if G.M., themselves, manage to become 100% compliant — this includes a staggering 2 billion lines of code plus hundreds of thousands of embedded chips — how about their 85,000 suppliers? Have we not often seen a strike in one GM component plant cripple the entire operation within a week? And, will it not be the same with any supplier? How can you make a car without rubber, textiles, glass, plastic or steel? If any one supplier fails to deliver their specific part or material, it will bring the entire operation to a halt. This is the domino effect!

Just In Time Inventorying.

The never ending quest for profitability and cost effectivity has resulted in the concept of *"just in time" (JIT)* inventorying.

Pioneered by Toyota in the late '60s, *JIT* inventorying did away with the existing practice of stocking a ninety day supply of *all* materials necessary to maintain the manufacturing process. Instead, material is brought to the factory, *as needed*. All is dependant upon delivery by truck, train or air, and is precisely timed and entirely computer controlled. Any interruption in this precisely timed flow of material will stop everything and cause massive unemployment and shortages.

Even our food supply incorporates *JIT* deliveries, with perishable foods being brought into the cities on a daily basis. No supermarket stocks more than a 72 hour supply of food, assuming that everyone buys as per normal! What will happen when more people become concerned about Y2k and start stocking up on foodstuffs? How long will supplies then last?

Our Most Precious Resource.

Without doubt, our most precious modern resource is electricity! Our entire existence depends upon it; it is the lifeblood of our civilization. Without electricity, we can't even fix the computer systems that fail!

The Electric Power Grid.

All of North America is connected together in a computer controlled electric power grid. As the power demand increases in an area, more is directed to it from other areas where demand is lower. However, as we have seen more than a few times in past decades, a minor problem in one area can take out large portions of this grid.

For instance, in August, 1996, power was disrupted for several hours in fourteen Western states and two Canadian provinces when a high voltage line sagged onto a tree in Oregon! The resulting power outage affected four million customers over 1.8 million square miles! A similar power outage happened a month earlier in Idaho, affecting 1.5 million customers in eight states and parts of Canada.

Previous to these two events, one of the last major outages was in the North Eastern U.S. and Canada back in 1965. That outage left 30 million people without power for a full 13 hours!

This power outage was due to a tripped overload relay in Niagara Falls, N.Y.; whereas, both of the Western events were initiated by sagging powerlines touching trees. The main point here, however, is that the power grid is *vulnerable* and is susceptible to wide area outages as a result of failures of equipment or events elsewhere.

To further demonstrate the reliability, or lack thereof, of the system, transmission and distribution power outages cost U.S. businesses an estimated $29 billion annually in lost productivity *without* any Y2k related problems!

What Are We Up Against?

The North American power grid has often been called the *"largest machine ever devised by man"*. It incorporates over 200 bulk electric control centers which constantly monitor supply and demand, over 600,000 miles of transmission wires, and over 3,200 electrical generation entities (*plants*), which feed electricity into the power grid. In addition, hundreds of control centers are used to manage sub-transmission and distribution systems.

Every aspect of this huge network is controlled by an energy management system, called Supervisory Control and Data Acquisition (*SCADA*). The entire system is highly dependent on microwave, telephone, VHF radio, and satellite communications. *All must work, and work perfectly!*

As of the time of this writing, *none* of these power generating entities, nor any of the communication links have *publicly* announced that they are 100% Y2k compliant, and time is now perilously short! Of those that have given any kind of public statement, none guarantee that the power will be on after January 1, 2000.

However, a recent report to the U.S. Department of Energy, by the North American Electric Reliability Council (*NERC*), states that 26% of non-nuclear and 32% of nuclear generation entities report completion of the remediation/testing phase. In other words, they feel that they have fixed and tested the problems they found. But, what is the status of the remaining 68-74% of electrical suppliers?

The vast majority (70%) of these critical utilities are just assessing the situation at this late date! It, therefore, seems obvious that power suppliers are failing to move rapidly enough on their Y2k repairs. This leaves us with no clear indication that the system will be reliably operating at the turn of the century!

Not only is the time remaining now perilously short, but we must also consider that the industry-wide repair effort is frustrated by not being able to easily shut down to do the necessary modifications and testing. In order to shut down a major generation station to do repairs a lot of planning must be done. Before it can be shut down, some other facility must be on stand-by to replace the power. This ensures that the sudden shortage won't cause major portions of the grid to overload and drop out.

Interdependence = Vulnerability!

The high level of interdependence within the grid means that the strength of the system is only as strong as its weakest link. How many power plants have to fail to bring down major portions of the grid or even the entire grid? Will the expected failure of emergency services such as the police, fire and ambulances, force closure of the nuclear plants for safety reasons? If so, how will 118 nuclear plants going off-line affect operation of the North American power grid? How many will be forced to go off-line because of non-compliancy?

Most coal-fired plants only stock a one month supply of coal. Will the almost certain failure of the railway system shut down most of the *operating* coal-fired generation plants within a month after 2000? How will the failure of numerous coal-fired plants affect the grid?

The following breakdown shows how electricity is generated in North America:

— U.S.A —

- burning coal supplies = 57%
- nuclear supplies = 20%
- hydro generation = 11%
- gas, oil, geothermal = 12%

— Canada —

- hydro generation = 64%
- burning coal = 19%
- nuclear = 16%
- other = 1%

— Mexico —

- coal/natural gas/oil = 68%
- hydro generation = 25%
- nuclear = 4%

Most electrical generation comes from burning coal and is, therefore, totally dependant upon the railroad system. But, at this time, not one railroad is compliant! The routing and scheduling of trains is one of the most date-sensitive and computer-dependent programs known, and yet they are years away from proven compliancy.

In addition, over past decades, the railways have done away with manual switching and switching yards in favor of computerized switching on the fly. The ability to revert to manual operation no longer exists. If the computers fail, the railway fails!

The railway is totally dependent on electricity and the electricity is totally dependent on the railways. And, all is dependent upon reliable data communications!

Every single aspect of our modern society is controlled by a complex, sophisticated network of interlinked and interdependent computers. A network of computers destined to fail, because we, and our political and business leaders, have failed to act in time!

Unfortunately, these computers are necessary for the production and delivery of the food we eat, the water we drink, the electricity that makes everything work, our jobs, all manufacturing and industry, transportation, government, banking, and all communications. In short, everything that supports modern life!

Other Indicators.

If there won't be any problems, why has President Clinton spent so much time passing executive orders that will give the government absolute control? Why have the Royal Canadian Mounted Police cancelled all vacations starting on December 27, 1999 until March 15, 2000? Could it perhaps be that they know something is afoot?

The best advice is to *"Hope for the best, but prepare for the worst." It is reasonable to expect that we are about to experience some major changes. What will you choose to do? Will you prepare or panic?*

Living Without Electricity

Nobody can be absolutely certain, if or for how long, the electricity will be off in any given area. But when we consider the complexity and all-pervading nature of the Y2k computer date problem, and the extreme dependence of the electrical generation system upon communications, railways, oil and fuel supplies and thousands of other suppliers, *the wise will prepare* for major, extended electric power outages.

We are preparing to live without electricity for at least six months and suggest that you do likewise. We hope and pray that the system will not fail, but strongly suspect that it will be off between one and six months. We don't, however, think it will be off much longer than six months, as restoration of the electricity will be everyone's top priority. It is, after all, our most vital resource!

Different Areas – Different Needs.
When Y2k descends upon the world in its full fury, it will, of course, be January 1, 2000. In southern parts of the world, it will be the very beginning of summer, whereas in the north it will be the very beginning of winter. But, no matter where you are in the world, you should expect frequent and lengthy power failures.

Those in the south will be more concerned with food spoilage than with heat, whereas those in the north will be more concerned about heat than with food spoilage. However, no matter where you are, you will want some means of cooking your food, brewing a tea or coffee, or purifying water for drinking and cooking needs. You will also appreciate some form of lighting for the nights, and if you're in the north (*winter*), you will definitely want some type of room heating.

When it comes to selecting heating, lighting and cooking equipment, your personal decision on exactly how you provide for yourself and your family depends upon many factors, factors such as: climate, what you live in (*house, apartment, condominium, or townhouse*), how serious you personally believe the Y2k problem will be, available room for fuel storage, the number of people you must provide for, and — as always — finances.

If you live in an apartment, where and how much fuel can you safely store? What are the local bylaws on fuel storage where you live? Common sense alone tells us that no fire department wants a lot of people in apartment buildings, each storing a couple of hundred gallons of volatile fuel! But, one thing is certain — if you don't store fuel for it, your new campstove is nothing more than an expensive paperweight!

Ultimately, each person needs to decide which is more important: personal survival for you and your family, or strict compliance with prevailing fuel storage regulations. The decision is yours!

If, however, you do decide to store enough fuel for 1 to 6 months, store it safely. Don't store fuel in a hot place, or near electrical equipment or any open flame. Make sure that the cans or cylinders are in good condition and the caps or valves are tight. If you smell fuel or gas, find the culprit and dispose of it immediately. Keep all fuel safely away from children. Always store fuel in *approved* containers; do not simply fill an old, plastic bleach bottle with gas and put it in your basement.

Be imaginative in your fuel storage. Where and how much fuel can you store? Can you store fuel off-site without having it stolen? Is there a nearby garden shed? Could it be buried in containers in the back yard and dug up as needed?

How Much to Store?

Since the fuel needs of those caught by Y2k in the summertime will be less than of those enduring winter, let's deal with winter. Room heating will be the number one fuel consumer. If you intend to heat your whole house or apartment, you will probably need more than one heater and a lot of fuel.

Estimate fuel needs by taking into account the burn rates of your heater(s), the size of the area you want to heat and the estimated time the heater will be used each day. Then multiply that figure by the number of days you expect to use the heater(s). Burn rates are usually published in the operation manual or in company catalogues.

If you are heating a house, you might want to consider a kerosene heater. There are many excellent models available. Kerosene fuel, however, cannot be used in most campstoves or mantle lamps, so be careful not to mix fuels. *Consult the operating manuals of your equipment*.

When doing the research for this book, I contacted Jeff Manning of Manning Service, Inc. in Indiana, for information on heating with kerosene. He uses a Toyostove DC 100 heater as the main source of heat in his home and uses just over 300 gallons of kerosene through the long, cold Indiana winter. The Toyostove heater adequately heats a 700 sq. foot area.

Kerosene is a safe fuel to store (*a lit match can be thrown into an open container of kerosene without igniting the kerosene*). If you own your own home you can safely and easily store enough kerosene to keep warm and comfortable for a few months.

I cannot apologize for the fact that without some form of fuel there can be no heat. So, if you are to survive on your own, you will need to store some kind of fuel.

The alternative is to go into some kind of community shelter. The military and emergency services do fairly well during emergencies like earthquakes or hurricanes, but how are they going to fare when the emergency is *everywhere and all at the same time*? Are their resources going to be stretched beyond the breaking point? Where are they going to get *their* supplies from?

A practical solution for the apartment dweller might be to use one of the dual mantle lamps as a source of heat as well as light. Note, however, that the labels on the lamp itself clearly warn not to use as a heat source! The label also cautions not to use indoors or even in a tent. Upon consultation with engineers, I have been assured of the following:

- The main reason for these cautions is for liability purposes as there is always a danger of fire or carbon monoxide poisoning when using any open flame.
- The carbon monoxide output from a properly maintained lamp (*i.e. no holes in the mantles*) is very small — in fact, almost negligible.
- The average dual mantle lamp gives off about 3,500 to 4,000 BTU's of heat — enough heat for a small room.
- For many hundreds of years, oil lamps, candles, kerosene lamps, gas lamps, and later, mantle lamps were the standard and only source of lighting in every home.

So, ***for liability purposes***, our advice is: don't ever use *any* open flame device indoors. If you do decide to use them indoors, you do so entirely at your own risk. And, if you do use them indoors, make absolutely sure that the room is well ventilated with a supply of fresh air and that you have a *battery operated* carbon monoxide detector in good working condition. Test your carbon monoxide and smoke detectors often.

To conserve fuel, you might want to consider withdrawing into and heating only one room. Put all the bedding, mattresses and pillows into that one room and dress warmly. This will conserve much fuel. Do keep in mind that you are *surviving*, not trying to maintain your normal lifestyle! However, be extremely careful not to start a fire.

Fuel Types.

When considering the purchase of any camping type equipment, two main fuel types are most common: **camp fuel** (*also known as Coleman fuel, or iosol*) and **propane**. Of the two fuels, propane is the cleanest burning and easiest to use; the flame is consistent, there is no messy fuel to bother with and it is not necessary to continually pump up the pressure on the tank.

Propane is a bit more expensive than liquid fuel, and is especially expensive when it comes to storing large quantities, because of the cost of the refillable pressure tanks necessary for storage.

Gas Lamp with 2 Mantles.

Specifications indicate that the dual mantle lamp will operate *up to* 14 hours on a full tank of camp fuel (2 pint/0.95 liter). It should then operate continually for 2.3 days on a 1 gallon can of fuel (3.8 liters). You normally would not operate the lamp continually unless you were also using it as a heat source. Burning 20 hours a day gives the following consumption rates:

Period	Fuel Consumed
1 day	3 pints/1.5 liters
1 week	2.6 gallons/10 liters
1 month	10.4 gallons/40 liters
6 months	62 gallons/240 liters

If the lamp were used for lighting *only* and burned for about six hours each day, it would use the following quantities of fuel:

Period	Fuel Consumed
1 day	1 pint/0.95 liter
1 week	1 gallons/4 liters
1 month	4 gallons/16 liters
6 months	24 gallons/96 liters

The discrepancy in estimated fuel consumption levels between the above two charts is accounted for by considering that the lamp burning continually will burn at the lowest level for 14 hours and at the highest for 6, whereas the lamp used for lighting *only* will be at the highest.

Two Burner Gas Campstove.

This two burner campstove will operate for 2 hours on a single tank of fuel (2 pints/0.95 liters), with both burners on high. It's unlikely that you would use the stove more than 4 hours each day for all your cooking and water purification needs.

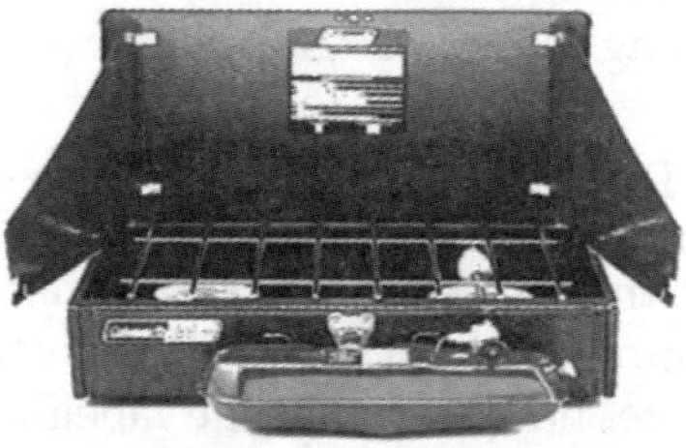

Period	Fuel Consumed
1 day	4 pints/2 liters
1 week	3.5 gallons/13 liters
1 month	14 gallons/52 liters
6 months	84 gallons/312 liters

Single Burner Gas Stove.

A more compact, easier to store model might be the single burner campstove. The tank holds 1.1 pint or 1 liter of fuel and burns for 1.75 hours with the burner on high. Great for one pot meals or for the single person. It will use slightly less fuel than one burner on the two burner model as it has closer contact to the pot and a more sheltered flame. If you only cook with it for about 4 hours each day, your fuel consumption will be not quite half that of the two burner stove.

Liquid Fuel Accessories.

Be sure to buy a replacement globe for your mantle lamp and a spare set of mantles. It might be a good idea to purchase a spare generator for both lamp and campstove. Also, make sure that you buy one of the filter funnels used to fill both the lamp and the stove. The filter funnel keeps dirt and other matter out of the fuel and prevents blockages.

Dual Mantle Propane Lamp.

Propane lamps such as this one, can operate off the small 16.4 oz cylinders as shown, or if you prefer, you can purchase the necessary adapters and run both your light and campstove from a 20 lb. refillable container.

A dual mantle lamp will burn for up to 18 hours on one 16.4 oz. cylinder.

These lamps also give off 3,500 to 4,000 BTU's of heat, and if burned 20 hours per day will consume the following quantities of propane:

Period	Fuel Consumed
1 day	21.8 oz. propane
1 week	10 lbs. propane
1 month	2 – 20 lb. tanks
6 months	8 – 20 lb. tanks

Again, if burned 20 hours per day as a heat source, the lamp will usually be turned to the lowest light level for at least 14 hours per day and will burn at the highest light level for 6 hours and off for 4 hours each day. If a lamp is used only as a light source, it will burn about 6 hours per day, but at the highest light level. It will then consume the following:

Period	Fuel Consumed
1 day	8.2 oz. propane
1 week	3.58 lbs. propane
1 month	14.5 lbs. propane
6 months	5 – 20 lb. tanks

Two Burner Propane Stove.

With both burners on high this stove will last up to 4.5 hours on a 16.4 oz. cylinder of propane.

Using both burners an average of four hours cooking per day should take care of all your cooking and water purification needs. You will then consume the following quantities of propane:

Period	Fuel Consumed
1 day	14.6 oz. propane
1 week	6 – 16.4 oz. cylinders
1 month	27 lbs. propane
6 months	8 – 20 lb. tanks

Fuel quantities should be sufficient, but each person or group of persons will use less or more fuel depending upon circumstances, lifestyle, and personal desires.

Please exercise the maximum in caution and safety practises with fuel storage and in how you use your lamps and stoves. Your life and the lives of others can depend upon what you do. Above all, use common sense — you cannot have 4 or 5 people living in a small room with a burning lantern and not have a constant fresh air supply.

Ensure that volatile heating fuels are not stored near the heater, and do not refuel the unit while it is running. Do not use oil lanterns, heaters, stoves or candles near flammable items such as furniture, clothing, curtains and other combustibles. And, make sure you have a carbon monoxide detector.

Kerosene Lantern.
A kerosene lamp will burn for about 12 hours on a quart of kerosene or lamp oil. The wicks will last for about 1000 hours, and the light will equate to a 40 watt light bulb. Burning the lamp 5 hours per day will use about 19 gallons of fuel over a six month period.

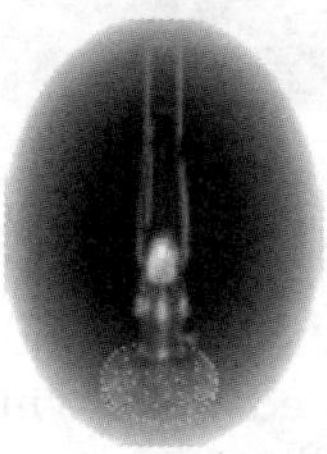

Flashlight.
The average flashlight will give continuous light for 5 to 6 hours when the batteries are new. It shouldn't be considered as your primary light source, but you shouldn't be without one. Even in emergencies — emergencies do happen.

If you can, purchase batteries from one of the wholesale bulk outlets, and be sure to get a spare bulb or two. Avoid rechargeable batteries, as the power may be off!

Battery Operated Fluorescents.
Some of the modern fluorescent lamps give adjustable levels of light. Again however, avoid those with rechargeable batteries for the same reason. The larger lamps operate on 8 D-cell batteries. They will operate from 16 to 20 hours on low, 8 to 12 hours on high, depending on the model. Most have a night light which will run for 110 hours on a set of batteries.

Candles.
Always good to keep a few of these around, both in the home and in the car. In a roadside emergency a candle can provide a surprising amount of warmth, even to the extent of keeping a person from freezing, if trapped overnight in a car in winter. Keep an open tin can in the car to safely hold the candle as it burns. Candles are available in a wide variety of sizes and shapes, but most of the normal emergency candles are about 4″ high and ¾″ in diameter. Depending on the quality of the wax they will burn for 3 to 4 hours. Most inexpensive candles are made of a mixture of paraffin wax and stearin *(for a brighter light)*. You can buy them just about anywhere.

Sterno Fuel.

A jelled fuel in a can. Available at most hardware stores and sporting stores. Comes in two main styles, with or without a wick. The wick type offers a little more control over the temperature than the open flame type. Each can burns for about 2 hours and is suitable for warming and cooking. You must purchase or devise a metal stand that sits over the burning fuel cannister and supports the pot or pan. There should be about 1½" to 2" of space between the can and the pot.

Wood Burning.

If you are one of those fortunate souls who already has a wood stove in your home, you need to consider laying in enough wood to heat and to cook with for at least six months. Depending on your particular stove, 8 to 12 face cords of wood should be adequate for six months of continual burning. The amount of wood needed depends on many factors: type of stove, kind of wood, how wet the wood is and how hot you want to keep your home.

If your home doesn't have a wood burning stove, you might want to consider installing one. You can choose from a wide variety of modern airtight stoves, Franklin stoves, box stoves or even a fireplace. It is wisest to get a stove that will allow you to cook your meals as well as heat your home.

It is easy to cook on any of these stoves, but fireplaces are another matter altogether, as the metal hooks that were once commonly used to suspend the heavy cast-iron pots are no longer a standard feature on the modern fireplace. You can, however, easily devise a metal tripod using a metal chain and "S" hook to suspend pots over the coals.

If you have a fireplace in your home, you must analyze it very carefully before you bet your life on what it can do. Some fireplaces are used for decorative purposes only and any kind of *real* fire will cause damage.

Do not, under any circumstances, try to build a wood fire in any fireplace designed for natural gas or propane! A wood fire in these fireplaces will damage the flu, the metal chimney, the fireplace itself, perhaps cause an explosion, and will exhaust more noxious fumes into the house than out of the chimney. A wood fire is simply too hot for the light construction of the average gas fireplace!

Many modern fireplaces or wood furnaces incorporate an electric fan to circulate the hot air into the room. But, if the electricity is off, will the heat of a wood fire without the fan cause hot spots, melt downs and even start a fire? You should contact a fireplace specialist well before January 1, 2000, to learn all that you can about safely using your fireplace.

Fireplaces are notorious for being inefficient, often giving less than 10% heating efficiency compared to upward of 60% efficiency for the best airtight stove. For maximum fireplace efficiency, make effective use of your damper — a hinged piece of metal in the throat of the chimney that controls the flow of air up the chimney. Fully open the damper when starting the fire, but once the fire is burning, close it down to the smallest possible opening without causing the release of smoke into the room. This reduces the volume of *already heated* room air being lost up the chimney. Fully close the damper when the fire is out. But, make sure it is completely out or smoke will fill the room. Also, it would be wise to have your chimney cleaned in preparation for a season of intensive use.

And, of course, don't forget the tools necessary for cutting and splitting the wood *(axes, splitting mauls or wedges, Swede saw, etc.)*. Be sure to have on hand the files or grinding stones you will need to keep these tools sharp. If you use one, keep a spare blade for your Swede saw.

You might have a gas chain saw. If you do, get a spare cutting chain and spark plug, sharpening jig and files. You will also need to store a few gallons of gas and enough oil to mix in the gas, as well as some chain oil to prevent the chain bar from being damaged from the heat and friction of the chain.

The most important thing is your wood supply. Make sure that your calculations take into account that it may be your only heat source, and that you will be using it all day and all night. If possible, you may want to store your wood inside. It will keep the wood dry and will prevent theft!

Safety — Carbon Monoxide.

Without electricity, most of us will be forced to heat, cook and provide light with some kind of open flame device, and that subjects us to the inherent dangers of carbon monoxide poisoning.

We recommend that everyone purchase a *battery operated* carbon monoxide detector. Buy 2 if you can afford them, one for your cooking area and the other for your sleeping area. Avoid models that plug in or are hard-wired, as they will be useless when the power goes off. Be sure also to purchase a spare battery for each.

Carbon monoxide is a colorless, odorless, tasteless and dangerous gas. It is a by-product from the *incomplete burning* of carbon-based fuels such as coal, gasoline, iosol or camp fuel, kerosene, oil and wood.

Don't take carbon monoxide poisoning lightly — over 100 people were hospitalized by it, and 9 died from it, during the January '98 ice storm power outage in Quebec, Ontario and parts of the North Eastern U.S.. These people experienced what it was like to be without electricity for about 3 to 6 weeks in the beginning of winter — exactly when Y2k will strike the northern countries. We can learn much from their experience.

Carbon monoxide detectors do have limitations. Some people, such as the elderly, infants and those challenged by breathing or heart problems, are at increased risk from even low levels, and may experience symptoms well before a detector sounds the alarm.

In addition, some detectors may not give adequate warning if carbon monoxide levels increase too rapidly *(15 minutes or less)* to a very high level. These high levels would probably only be achieved by running an automobile in a closed garage or a gasoline electric generator indoors. During the January, '98, ice storm, fear of having their electric generators stolen prompted some people to run their generators indoors. Some paid dearly for their caution!

Carbon monoxide poisoning symptoms can include dizziness, nausea, headache, weakness, loss of muscle control, chest tightness, heart fluttering, sleepiness, redness of the skin, confusion, vomiting and diarrhea. Caution: often people think they have the flu when, in reality, they are suffering from CO poisoning.

Carbon monoxide poisoning should be suspect if more than one member of the family is sick and if they feel better after being away from home for a period of time.

People who suspect they are being exposed to carbon monoxide, should immediately seek fresh air and tend to whatever device might be the source of the carbon monoxide. All gas flames should be blue in color. A yellow flame or a flame that is excessively high, noisy and sputtering indicates improper combustion, and can give off high levels of carbon monoxide. Never use charcoal barbecue grills to cook or heat inside the home — not even in a fireplace!

Safety — The Danger of Fire.

Fire is the third leading cause of accidental death in the United States, and yet, most people completely ignore the danger. Y2k, however, is going to greatly increase the risk of death and property loss by fire, by forcing us to return to the use of fire to cook with, and to heat our homes. Therefore, an important part of our survival preparation is to be ready to deal with those increased risks.

We can prepare by recognizing that there are increased risks, and by equipping ourselves to quickly detect and effectively fight any fire that might occur. We need to determine what kind of fire might be encountered, and the type of extinguisher that would be needed to fight that fire.

Begin by placing a *battery operated* smoke detector with fresh batteries in any area where there is a risk of fire. Again, don't purchase the plug-in or hard-wired models as they will be useless when the power goes off. Do keep a spare battery for each.

Types of Fires.

There are four classifications of fires, but for our purposes, we will only be concerned with three of them, class A , class B and class C.

Class A fires involve ordinary combustibles or fibrous material, such as wood, paper, cloth, rubber and some plastics. Most of these types of materials are readily found in the home.

Class B fires involve combustible liquids such as gasoline, kerosene, Coleman fuel, iosol and propane. This encompasses all the fuels we will be storing for survival.

Class C fires involve energized electrical equipment, such as appliances, panel boxes, switches and power tools. We won't have any problems with class C fires when the power is off, but could have a problem when it comes back on. When the power fails, you should turn off all the subfeed breakers to prevent damage to appliances from power surges when it comes back on.

Personally, I would leave the main breaker on and one 15 amp breaker that feeds lights in the living room or dining room. By leaving a switch on for a light fed by that circuit, you will know the instant power is restored. Tape the switch in the on position to avoid having it accidentally turned off.

The Proper Extinguisher.

The rating of the extinguisher is shown on the extinguisher faceplate. Most are marked with multiple ratings such as AB, BC or ABC. These extinguishers are capable of putting out more than one classification of fire. The ABC type extinguisher will deal with all of our Y2k fire needs. Make sure you keep one handy.

Prevention is Best.

It's a lot easier to prevent fires than it is to have to fight one! So don't take chances. Keep combustible materials away from burning lamps, heaters and stoves. Store fuels only in approved containers and safely away from heat or open flames. Don't refuel lamps, heaters or stoves in a confined space, especially near an open flame. Don't refuel lamps or heaters when they are still hot.

Points to Remember.

If the fire is threatening your path of escape or if your extinguisher is exhausted of agent, then leave the area immediately. Stay low to avoid smoke and toxic gases; since the best air is close to the floor, crawl if necessary.

Water — Is It Safe To Drink?

You Can't Live Without Water.

In a survival situation, water is the one thing you absolutely cannot live without. The human body is fully 60% water, with water being critically important for every single metabolic function within the body. You might live for up to sixty days without solid food, but you will only live for several days without water. In fact, with no water intake whatsoever *(including none from food)*, three or four days is the longest we can live.

It's easy to take water for granted! Most of the time we fail to realize how much water we need, because we also get much needed fluids from the foods we eat. And as city dwellers, we rightly expect to get all the water we need simply by turning a faucet handle.

However, what happens if the power goes off for weeks or even months because of Y2k computer glitches? Where, from within your city, will you find a safe, reliable source of water to drink, cook and wash with?

We can be quite confident that the supermarket shelves will be empty long before the crunch, so buying bottled water probably won't be an option. Adequate *preparation* is the only answer, if we are to ensure that we and our families have the necessary water supplies to see us through the difficult times ahead.

So What Can We Do?

If there is even a chance that we might be caught without water, we must prepare. And, we must prepare *before* it happens. Our only options are to either find an alternative source of water or to store enough to meet our daily needs.

Water Storage.

Storing water is probably one of the quickest and easiest ways to ensure a safe supply of water. It is especially easy if it is done *before* the electricity goes out. To prepare beforehand, all you have to do is obtain enough food-grade containers and fill them using a plastic garden hose *(rubber hoses will leave an aftertaste)*.

If you don't prepare in advance, you will cause yourself much hardship later on. You will have to scrounge the containers, try to find a source of safe, unpolluted water, and lug the water filled containers from the source to your home — perhaps even through crowds of angry, desperate, thirsty people who don't have any containers of their own! You will also have to pay dearly for the containers and perhaps even the water as the prices are certain to increase when supplies become limited.

Water can be safely stored for many years if it is stored in food-grade containers, is free of bacteria and is kept in a cool, dark place.

How you store your water supply will largely be determined by where you live. If you live in your own home or townhouse, your basement will provide a ready place for water storage. If you live in an apartment, you will have a different set of challenges.

Generally, the best arrangement is to obtain at least one, preferably two, large storage containers which you will use to store your primary source of water. You can then siphon water into a smaller, easier to manage container or bucket as needed.

It is advisable to have two primary water storage containers in case one develops a leak or somehow becomes contaminated. Water storage containers come in just about any size. The size you choose will be determined by the storage space available to you, the length of time you want to provide for, the number of people you are storing water for, and finances available.

How Much do we Need to Store?

In very serious survival situations, life has been sustained on as little as one pint of water per day, but that small amount of water is not enough to support life indefinitely. A more realistic survival amount would be one gallon per person per day, which will provide for your basic drinking and cooking needs *only*. You might be able to squeeze the odd, occasional sponge bath in as well.

Four gallons per day per person will allow for personal hygiene, and the washing of a few dishes. Ten to fifteen gallons of water will even allow for a few well-planned toilet flushes throughout the day. *Hint: put some tape over the flush handle to avoid those habitual, thoughtless flushes.*

When water is plentiful the modern city dweller can use as much as 150 gallons per day. Most of this water normally goes down the drain through toilet flushes, showers and letting the water run as we brush our teeth or wash dishes. Under survival conditions, life is very different.

How Bad is it Going to Be?

We can only guess how much chaos the Y2k issue is going to bring into our lives. Without any doubt, the most crucial issue — the one with the greatest impact on our lives — will be the supply of electricity. It, and it alone, will determine whether or not we have a convenient supply of water.

Predictions of electrical disruptions range from no down time at all to complete meltdown with the power grid being down for a year or longer!

Personally, I believe that we need to store water for *at least* three months and food for *at least* six months to a full year. The more you store, the greater will be your survivability and the greater your peace of mind.

So, What About Containers?

Your choice of containers will be determined by your personal situation. Containers are available from a 50,000 gallon collapsible water tank right on down to a one liter water bottle.

Give careful consideration to your needs and the needs of your family and available storage area. Those of you who own your own home have a much greater range of options than those of us who live in apartments. We apartment dwellers must, of necessity, be more creative in how we store and provide water.

Probably the most convenient storage container for the apartment dweller is the 55 gallon plastic drum. They can be brought in empty, set in place and filled by a hose connected to your water faucet — if the water from your faucet is good enough to drink! *In our area, the water we get from the tap is drinkable, but unpleasant, so I am buying reverse osmosis water in 5 gallon containers and filling the large drums. Tedious and expensive, but worth it in the end.*

Plan where you are going to place your drums. Water weighs 8 lbs. per gallon, so the filled drums will weigh 440 lbs each. You don't want to be moving them around. If you store them in the same place, make sure the floor can support the combined weight of all the full drums. Make sure that your containers are food grade. *Hint: Don't make the mistake of buying new plastic garbage cans and filling them with water, as chemicals will leech from the container into the water over time.*

Other Sources of Containers.

The largest soft drink bottles are excellent storage containers. They can be filled and stacked just about anywhere, including under the bed! Just make sure they don't leak. Some boxes from the liquor store will perfectly hold six full bottles, allowing you to stack them conveniently in the basement.

Often, you can purchase large bulk containers from restaurants or fast food places. They get food items like ice cream, yogurt or mayonnaise in 2 or 3 gallon containers with tight sealing, snap-on lids. *Caution: They will be in high demand as more people start preparing, and sometimes they can leech a taste into the water, depending on what was in the container. Avoid using any container that retains a strong odor after being thoroughly washed. Also beware of the biodegradable plastic containers sometimes used for milk or distilled water as they will break down in six months!*

Making it All More Convenient.

Purchase a 10 foot length of ½"I.D. *(internal diameter)* clear Tygon tubing to use as a siphon. This may become one of your most precious and useful tools, as you will use it to transfer water from the large containers to a smaller, more convenient-to-carry container. Most hardware stores will carry this type of tubing. *Hint: you will need a longer siphon if you stack your drums. You will need the additional length so you can siphon out of the barrels that are stacked on the top.*

Keep your siphon clean. Mark the end that goes into the water so that you can distinguish it from the end you suck on to get the flow going. Clean after every use in water mixed with a little bleach. *Hint: with a knife, cut a small notch in the end that goes into the water. Also, don't use your water siphon for any other fluid transfer (i.e. gasoline)!*

We purchased an inexpensive hand pump that fits on the top of one of the standard 5 gallon water containers. It sits in our kitchen and we use it for all our drinking and cooking needs. It works well and is a convenient setup. When you empty the 5 gallon jug, siphon more water from one of the drums.

Treating Stored Water.

Water stored for relatively short terms (*3 to 6 months*) shouldn't need to be treated to maintain its purity. *If* it was clean, bacteria-free water and was put into clean containers, kept cool and stored in a dark place it should be safe to drink. That's probably the only good thing about the Y2k issue — we know exactly when it is going to happen, and therefore, know when to begin storing water.

Most city dwellers — including myself — don't want to permanently adopt the *"survivalist"* life style, and aren't wanting to store water for 10 to 20 years or longer. It is prudent and wise, however, to prepare in this particular instance, as the likelihood of major disruptions in our water supply is almost certain.

What if it Lasts Much Longer?

If the power and water are off for periods longer than 3 months, then we are in a really critical survival situation. If this happens, you can be sure that your every waking moment will be totally consumed by providing protection and the basic needs for you and your family. The only thing that will help you then, is adequate preparation — *NOW!*

If the electricity and, therefore, the water supply are off for extremely long periods of time, you will find yourself using the nearest river, lake, pond or spring as a water source. This is where your risk of getting contaminated or polluted water, and the possibility of illness or disease increases greatly.

When we scrounge water in an emergency situation, our primary concern must be the quality of the water. Can we drink it safely? For if we aren't careful here, we run the risk of picking up some extremely debilitating diseases — diseases that can lay us up for weeks or months or even lead to death!

Caution: The E.P.A. estimates that over 90% of the world's surface water is unsafe to drink, if untreated!

As a safeguard, consider purchasing one of the small microfilter pumps that many experienced backpackers carry. They come in many different qualities, sizes, capacities and price ranges. And, if our modern society degrades to this extent, you will appreciate the mobility these units will provide.

Most use either ceramic, carbon, paper or glass fiber filter cartridges to filter out impurities. All models filter coarse organic material out of the water, some filter out protozoa and bacteria, as well. I am, however, cautious of companies that claim their filter will remove viruses, as the smallest common filter pore size is 0.2 microns, and viruses range from .02 to .25 microns in diameter. Some viruses will be filtered out, but you cannot guarantee that you will get all of them.

We purchased a microfilter pump with a cleanable 0.2 micron ceramic filter cartridge and a large capacity *(As much as 10,000 gallons/ 50,000 liters before filter replacement is necessary)*.

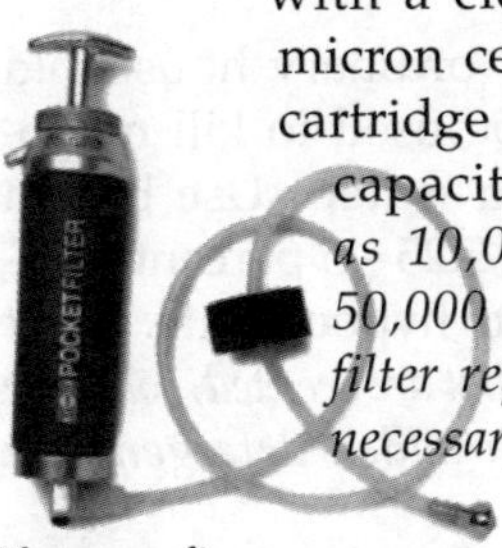

If your finances permit, buy two complete, identical pumps and two replacement cartridges, in case one breaks or is stolen. Also, parts from one can be used to fix the other. *Hint: these filter pumps will be extremely valuable, if Y2k wreaks this kind of havoc upon us!*

What is in Our Water?

Protozoa: Commonly found in 90% of the surface water in both Canada and the U.S.. Includes *Giardia* and *Cryptosporidium*. Range in size from 1 to 15 microns — easily filtered out by a 0.2 micron filter.

Bacteria: Organisms such as *E. coli, Campylobacter jejuni, Vibriocholera Shigella* and *Salmonella* cause such diseases as typhoid fever, cholera, diarrhea, and dysentery. Size: 0.2 to 10 microns. Easily filtered out with a 0.2 micron filter.

Viruses: In Canada and the United States we don't often encounter many viruses in our surface water, but this could change dramatically if Y2k problems force us to dump massive volumes of untreated human waste into the water system. Water-borne viruses cause illnesses such as hepatitis and polio.

Don't be tempted to drink untreated water because you've done it before and gotten away with it. Things change! Much depends upon the strength of your immune system, and even that changes from day to day. The best policy is to do everything you can to ensure the water that you drink, wash dishes in, cook with or brush your teeth with, is safe.

How Can We Make Water Safe?

The safest way to treat your water is to *boil* carefully *filtered* water that is taken from the cleanest water source you can find. *Boiling* is the only way to be absolutely certain that your water is free of pathogens *(harmful organisms)*.

Keep the water at a rolling boil for at least *3 minutes* to ensure that all harmful organisms are killed. Don't cut corners on the boil time, even if you are in a hurry, because sickness can be even more of an inconvenience.

You can improve the taste of boiled water if you put oxygen back into it by shaking it in a half full container or by pouring it back and forth from one clean container to another.

Chemical Treatment of Water.

Most city dwellers have many things in common, not the least of which is their proximity to large industrial centers, which, for many decades have dumped every conceivable type of waste into the water table. In addition, all cities must deal with massive quantities of human waste.

At the time of this writing, we live on the Niagara Peninsula between Lake Erie and Lake Ontario. This summer, *wherever* we took our dog — a Border Collie named Casey — for a swim, he broke out with a nasty, persistent bacterial skin condition within a day or two!

Somehow, the thought of going down to the same lake, scooping out a bucket of water, filtering it through a few old shirts or linens stretched over another bucket, then putting in a few drops of iodine, chlorine or bleach, and drinking the resulting mix, doesn't do much for either of us! Knowing how bad the water is, we could never feel good about drinking it unless we had done everything we could to ensure that it was safe.

We're much more comfortable with filtering the water through a fine ceramic filter and then boiling the water. But, in an emergency survival situation, chemicals do have their place in the treating of water, and not everyone will have a microfilter pump.

If you don't have a microfilter pump, do your best to filter the water through clean cloths and/or by letting it settle overnight. Siphon or ladle off the clear water from the top into a clean, tightly covered, noncorrosive container where it will then be disinfected. *Be careful not to draw any of the sediment from the bottom of the container.*

Bleach: Any ordinary household bleach can be used to kill microorganisms in water. Use bleach containing a 5.25 - 6 percent solution of sodium hypochlorite. *Don't use bleaches that are scented, colorsafe or those with added detergents or cleaners.*

Add 16 drops of bleach per gallon of water, mix thoroughly and let stand for 30 minutes before using. If the water doesn't have a slight bleachy odor, add 8 more drops per gallon, mix and let stand for an additional 15 minutes.

Iodine: Use 20 drops of 2% tincture of iodine per gallon of water. If the quality of the water is questionable, double the amount of iodine. Mix well and allow to stand for 30 minutes. *Caution:* don't use iodine if you are pregnant, nursing, or have a known thyroid condition.

12 percent sodium hypochlorite: Has outstanding disinfection properties. It has been proven by the Institute Pasteur in Paris, France, to be the most effective disinfectant against pathogenic bacteria, fungi and viruses. Widely used in homes, schools, hospitals, drinking water supplies, swimming pools, and for disinfecting hard surfaces and surgical instruments. This concentration is considered to be for industrial or institutional applications, so use carefully. Add 8 drops of 12% sodium hypochlorite solution to 1 gallon of water, as it is twice the strength of regular bleach. Available in most hardware stores or swimming pool supply stores.

Granular calcium hypochlorite: Mix 1 heaping teaspoon in 2 gallons of water to make a chlorine solution which can then be used to disinfect water. Use 2½ tablespoons of this solution to disinfect one gallon of water. Available in most hardware or swimming pool supply stores.

Commercial tablets: Use iodine or chlorine water purification tablets in accordance with directions on the package. These are available at most hardware or sporting goods stores.

Hydrogen Peroxide: Is an acceptable disinfectant for water, but is difficult to ensure that the right amount is used as residual levels need to be measured to ensure that disinfection is complete and that an overdose isn't being administered. To be accurate, dosages must be measured in parts per million *(ppm)*. So, unless you have the equipment to measure, you're probably better to leave this one alone.

Chemical Treatment Cautions.

Some controversy exists about using chemicals ***that do not*** contain sodium hypochlorite as the only active ingredient. For instance, F.E.M.A., the Federal Emergency Management Agency, doesn't recommend anything other than bleach or sodium hypochlorite as a method of chemically treating water.

Experts even caution that using chlorine or iodine to treat water doesn't guarantee that all giardia organisms are killed. Some even warn that they *(chlorine and iodine)* are totally ineffective against cryptosporidum.

Boiling is the **only** surefire way to ensure the safety of your drinking water. Unfortunately, this requires a heat source. Considering that the chances of your electricity being off because of Y2k related problems is extremely high, we highly recommend the purchase of a portable campstove and adequate fuel, and buy it *well before* January 1, 2000!

Distillation.
When the steam from boiling water hits a cool surface, it condenses back into water. This condensed water is free of harmful pathogens, salts and minerals. Distilled water is one of the purest, cleanest and safest forms of drinking water.

In a survival situation, a simple still can be devised as pictured below with items readily available within the home.

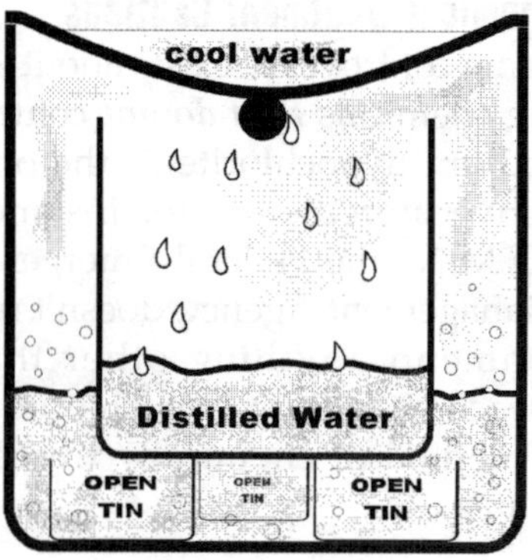

Take the largest, deepest, metal pot you can find and place a smaller pot inside on three ***opened,*** thoroughly cleaned tins *(tuna tin size).* ***Don't use unopened cans as they will explode!*** The idea is to have the inner pot elevated above the bottom of the larger pot, so that more of the unclean water can be put in the large pot to boil.

The inner pot should be high enough to ensure that the unclean boiling water doesn't splash into the distilled water. Place an inverted pot lid on the top of the large container. As the unclean water boils, the steam will hit the inverted lid, condense and drip into the inner pot. This will be pure, drinkable water.

To speed up the distillation process, put a bit of cold water in the inverted lid. As it warms, you can ladle it out and replace it with cooler water. Make sure, however, that the pot lid you use, doesn't allow the cooling water in the lid to drip through into the distilled water.

You can pour more unclean water into the outer pot during the boiling process, by carefully removing the lid with oven mitts.

So, Where Do We Find Water?
Much of this will be answered by how bad the Y2k problems will be; if all transportation is shut down and no gasoline is to be had, you will have to walk to the nearest source. That might be a river, a pond or a city fountain while supplies last.

If you do have gasoline and can drive, look in the yellow pages for the nearest spring water supplier. Hopefully they won't be down due to power outages.

Also, what are the possibilities of water wells in your area? Perhaps some old, abandoned wells can be reopened *(if possible, test the water before using, otherwise boil)?* Where is the nearest rural area where working wells may be found? Are there any nearby springs which supply good water throughout the year? *Caution: **ask for permission before taking water and be sure to respect the person's property — the life you save may be your own!***

Snow as a Water Source.

When Y2k descends upon us in its full fury, it will be winter in North America. This will be unfortunate because we will need fuel to heat our homes, but fortunate as we will have snow and ice as a source of water.

Fresh snow is the cleanest snow source and can just be melted and used. If, however, you use snow or ice that has been lying around for a while, you should boil it before you use it, as it can contain bacteria and organic material. Once it cools you may also want to run it through some form of filtration. ***Don't eat ice or snow,*** as it will chill you and cause a loss of energy, which will deplete you of vital body fluids. Your net fluid loss will far outweigh any liquid gained from eating snow or ice!

Riverbank Infiltration.

This is a water treatment process that exploits the river bank as a natural filter to improve water quality. Find a place next to a river where the ground level is only a foot or so above the water level. Fine sands or soils are best. Then dig a hole about 12 to 15 feet away from the edge of the river. The hole must be dug 3 to 5 feet lower than the level of water in the river *(shore up the sides of the hole with planks or shrubbery to prevent the walls from collapsing into the hole).*

The water that seeps into the hole should be free of pollutants and harmful pathogens, but it still won't hurt to boil the water so as to be absolutely safe. Be sure you aren't digging into a river bank that was created by the dumping of toxic industrial waste!

This might be a good community project in an emergency survival situation *(i.e. Y2k!)* Once a large enough hole is dug, the community may want to consider building an insulated shed over the hole to prevent it from freezing over. Depending on available resources, the building could even be heated.

Using the Sun to Melt Snow.

Suspend a black plastic garbage bag on two poles as shown. Put some clean snow or ice on the plastic and face it toward the sun. Tuck the end of the plastic into a jar so that the water can trickle in as it melts.

Be imaginative in your quest for water. It's surprising where you can find it and how innovative you can be in treating it.

Handy Water Related Tips

- To improve the flavor of stored or treated water, pour it from one clean container to another several times, or half fill a container and shake vigorously. This action will force oxygen into the water and improve the taste.
- Adding a few drops of bottled, concentrated lemon juice or powdered drinks like iced tea mix, Kool-aid or Tang will disguise unpleasant tastes in the water. But don't use this to disguise the bad taste of water, if you aren't positive that it is safe to drink.
- The quality of water that goes into a microfilter pump greatly influences how long the filter will last; you will shorten its life by filtering dirty water which contains a lot of organic matter. Tie a cloth or a paper coffee filter over the input hose, and keep it out of the dirt.
- When not in use, enclose the tip of the ***output hose*** in a plastic bag to prevent contamination. Run a solution of bleach water through your pump to clean it after every use. Keep at least one spare filter. Don't mistreat the pump — you can't afford to break it! Let your pump dry after using it.
- Use wisdom with your microfilter pump. Don't take it down to the water source and use it in front of others. You could be mugged or perhaps even murdered for your filter pump! Better to take untreated water home and use your filter pump in the privacy of your home.
- 1 gallon = 4 quarts/8 pints/16 cups/slightly less than 4 liters.
- A toboggan or sled will be handy to transport water in the winter.
- Carbon filtration devices can be used to remove unpleasant tastes like those in water disinfected by chlorine or iodine.
- In survival conditions you can conserve water by avoiding things such as alcohol, coffee, tea, tobacco and extremely salty foods. All cause dehydration and put a greater demand on limited water supplies.
- Never drink water from any source that contains remains of dead animals.
- Just because animals or birds drink from water doesn't necessarily mean that it is safe for human consumption. It may contain bacteria, viruses or parasites that cannot be neutralized by the human digestive tract.
- If your water supplies run low, cut down on the amount used, but **don't severely ration** your water. Use what you need today and try to find more tomorrow. The minimum water required to maintain bodily functions is 2½ quarts or 10 cups per person, per day.
- A full **rolling boil** refers to the stage when water *(or whatever)* is boiling so rapidly that you can't stir the boil down with a spoon.

Stocking Up — How Much?

For each person in your family, we suggest that you prepare *"care packages"* that will last between three and six months. This is based on the assumption it will likely take at least three months before some of these items are again available on store shelves. Having an extra three months supply or even more, will allow you to use cash on hand for more important things — like fresh food or fuel.

Keep in mind that disruptions caused by Y2k-related problems will affect the majority of countries at the very beginning of winter.

Remember to keep all baby or child care products and medications, as well as all adult medications and other products safely stored to prevent accidents or injuries to babies, toddlers or children.

(Amounts to have on hand are only approximate suggestions — base your buying on your current consumption patterns)

Memory Jogger for Babies.

- Baby care manual *(purchase one that illustrates basic development and shows how to treat possible minor injuries and ailments).*
- Baby food *(in glass jars) (3-6+ months' supply). (Also, plan for your growing baby's increasing need for more solid foods).*
- Baby powder *(2-3 containers).*
- Baby soap *(1-2).*
- Baby thermometer *(1-2).*
- Bottles and nipples *(have extra).*
- Colic relief *(ask your pediatrician).*
- Cough and cold relief *(ask your pediatrician).*
- Diapers *(determine from current use patterns. Disposables: plan for sizes your baby will likely grow into during the six month period. Note: cloth is economical and environmentally better; however, rinsing and washing them will be difficult if water supplies are interrupted).*
- Diaper rash ointment *(2 tubes).*
- Formula *(as your baby needs).*
- Insect repellent *(2) (type: for baby's only).*
- Liquid vitamin and mineral supplement *(3-6+ mo. supply).*
- Pabulum *(as your baby needs).*
- Pain relief *(for earache or headache; ask your pediatrician).*
- Pre-moistened towelettes *(12 bulk pkgs).*
- Shampoo *(1) (for babies only).*
- Skin lotion *(2-3).*
- Soothers *(3).*
- Sunscreen *(1-2) (type: for babies only – 15 SPF or better).*
- Teething biscuits *(3-6+ boxes).*
- Teething gel *(1-2 tubes).*
- Teething ring *(2).*
- Wash cloths *(10)*, bath towels *(3) (for each child).*

Also, get some warm baby clothes, blankets, infant-type sleeping bags, rain suits, hats, mittens, scarves and booties; also a variety of toys. In three to six months, babies go through a lot of changes — try to prepare in advance for each stage as best you can by anticipating their future needs.

Memory Jogger for Toddlers.

- Antibacterial liquid soap *(3).*
- Bar soap *(biodegradable) (4-6).*
- Chewable vitamin and mineral supplement *(3-6+ mo. supply).*
- Children's cold and cough relief *(ask your pediatrician).*
- Children's pain relief *(ask your pediatrician).*
- Comb and brush *(1 set).*
- Diapers and/or training diapers *(determine from current use patterns. Disposables: plan for sizes your baby will likely grow into over the six month period. Note: cloth is economical and environmentally better; however, rinsing and washing them will be difficult if water supplies are interrupted).*
- Insect repellent *(2-3) (type: for children only).*
- Pre-moistened towelettes *(12 bulk pkgs.).*
- Shampoo *(2)* and conditioner *(1) (type: for babies or children only).*
- Skin lotion *(2).*
- Sunglasses *(2 pair per child).*
- Sunscreen lotion *(1) (type: for children only – 15 SPF or better).*
- Teething biscuits *(6-8+ boxes).*
- Toothbrushes *(2 for each child — small and soft).*
- Toothpaste *(3 small).*
- Toys & picture books — *(get a good variety as these may prove to be their main source of entertainment for a number of months).*
- Wash cloths *(5),* hand towels *(3),* bath towels *(2) (for each child).*

Memory Jogger for Kids (3-12yrs).

- Antibacterial liquid soap *(3).*
- Bar soap *(biodegradable) (4-6).*
- Chewable vitamin and mineral supplement *(3-6+ month supply).*
- Children's cold and cough relief *(ask your pediatrician).*
- Children's pain relief *(ask your pediatrician).*
- Comb and brush *(1 set).*
- Conditioner for hair *(1).*
- Dental floss *(1).*
- Emery boards *(2 pkgs of 10).*
- Insect repellent *(2-3) (type: for children only).*
- Nail clippers or a pair of small scissors *(1).*
- Pre-moistened towelettes *(6-12 bulk pkgs).*
- Shampoo *(2).*
- Skin lotion *(2).*
- Sunglasses *(2 pair per child).*
- Sunscreen lotion *(2-3) (type: for children only – 15 SPF or better).*
- Toothbrushes *(2 for each child — small and soft).*
- Toothpaste *(3 small).*
- Toys, books and board games.
- Wash cloths *(5),* hand towels *(3),* bath towels *(2) (for each child).*

Memory Jogger for Teens.

- Acne soap and acne creams.
- Antibacterial liquid soap *(3).*
- Bar soap *(biodegradable) (4-6).*
- Comb and brush *(1 set).*
- Contact lenses *(spare pair or disposables) (base on current use).*
- Contact lens storage and cleaning solutions *(base on current use).*
- Contraceptives/condoms *(if applicable).*
- Conditioner for hair *(1).*

- Cosmetics *(enough to survive!)*
- Dental floss *(2).*
- Deodorant *(3-6).*
- Emery boards *(2 pkgs of 10).*
- Hair care items you consider essential *(color, gels, etc. Forget the electric blow-drier and curling iron!).*
- Insect repellent *(2-3) (type: adult).*
- Mouth wash *(2 large).*
- Nail clippers or a pair of small scissors *(1).*
- Pre-moistened towelettes *(6 bulk pkgs).*
- Safety razor *(2)* and extra blades *(16 at least, or base on current use or disposables for 3-6 months).*
- Scissors *(for trimming hair).*
- Shampoo *(2).*
- Shaving cream or gel *(base on current use).*
- Skin lotion *(2).*
- Sunglasses *(2 pair per person).*
- Sunscreen lotion *(2-3) (type: 15 SPF or better).*
- Tampons or sanitary napkins *(plan for 6 months).*
- Toothbrushes *(2).*
- Toothpaste *(3).*
- Toothpicks *(1-2 boxes per person).*
- Tweezers *(pointed and flat edge).*
- Vitamin and mineral supplement *(3-6+ months supply).*
- Wash cloths *(5)* hand towels *(3)* bath towels *(2) (per person).*

Memory Jogger for Adults.

- After shave *(base on current use).*
- Antibacterial liquid soap *(3).*
- Bar soap *(biodegradable) (4-6).*
- Comb and brush *(1 set).*
- Conditioner for hair *(2).*
- Contact lenses *(spare pair or disposables) (base on current use)*
- Contact lens storage and cleaning solutions *(base on current use).*
- Contraceptives/condoms *(if applicable).*
- Cosmetics *(enough to survive!)*
- Dental floss *(3).*
- Deodorant *(3-6 per person).*
- Emery boards *(2 pkgs of 10).*
- Eye glasses *(prescription) (at least one extra pair).*
- Hair care items you consider essential *(color, gel, etc. Forget the electric blow-drier and curling iron!).*
- Insect repellent *(2-3) (type: adult).*
- Miscellaneous items *(cotton-balls, Q-tips, etc.).*
- Mouth wash *(2 large).*
- Nail clippers or a pair of small scissors *(1).*
- Pre-moistened towelettes *(6 bulk pkgs).*
- Prescriptions *(any necessary medications) (Explain your Y2k concerns to your doctor).*
- Repair kit for glasses.
- Safety razor *(2)* and extra blades *(16 at least, or base on current use or get disposables for 3-6 months).*
- Scissors *(for trimming hair).*
- Sewing kit.
- Shampoo *(2).*
- Shaving cream or gel *(base on current use).*
- Skin lotion *(3).*
- Sunglasses *(2 pair per person).*
- Sunscreen lotion *(2-3) (type: 15 SPF or better).*
- Tampons or sanitary napkins *(plan for 6 months).*
- Toothbrushes *(2).*

- Toothpaste *(3-4)*.
- Toothpicks *(1-2 boxes per person)*.
- Tweezers *(pointed and flat edge)*.
- Vaseline *(1 jar per person)*.
- Vitamin and mineral supplement *(3-6+ months supply)*.
- Wash cloths *(5)*, hand towels *(3)*, bath towels *(2) (per person)*.

Just-in-Case Memory Jogger.

Have on hand, at least, some products for the relief of each of these common conditions. When you need it, you'll be glad you have it. In general, one product for the treatment of each condition should be sufficient for your family. Buy extra of those items you use often.

- ***Allergies:*** congestion, itchy eyes and throat, watery eyes, skin rash or hives.
- ***Eye care:*** allergies, itching, watery eyes, dry eyes, infections, red, irritated or strained eyes.
- ***Feminine care:*** for menopause, menstrual cramps, pregnancy, PMS, vaginal itching, water retention, yeast infections.
- ***Foot care:*** athelete's foot, blisters, corn and callouses.
- ***Illnesses:*** cold or flu symptoms, cough, congestion, fever relief.
- ***Infections:*** bacterial, fungal, ring or pin worms.
- ***Pain relief:*** burns, canker sores, cold sores, denture sores, hemorrhoids, insect bites/stings, sunburn, teething, toothache.
- ***Pain relief (internal):*** arthritis, backache, earache, headaches, muscle aches/strains.
- ***Poisoning:*** vomit inducer, activated charcoal tablets to absorb poisons.
- ***Prescriptions:*** at least a one month emergency supply of any medication you require.
- ***Scalp conditions:*** dandruff, lice, psoriasis, seborrhea.
- ***Skin conditions:*** acne, allergic rashes, athletic itch, bites or stings, burns, dry skin, dry lips.
- ***Special condition products:*** such as diabetic supplies, etc.
- ***Stomach and bowel problems:*** acid stomach, constipation, gas, dehydration, diarrhea, heartburn, hemorrhoids, indigestion, motion sickness, nausea, ulcers, upset stomach, vomiting.

Memory Jogger for Seniors.

Follow the *"adult"* list but exclude certain items you no longer require. However, don't forget these items, if they apply.

- Denture care items.
- Diabetic supplies.
- Extra batteries for hearing aids, wheelchairs or anything else that requires batteries.
- Extra heart or blood pressure medications and any other prescriptions you depend upon *(a 2 to 6 month supply) (Explain your Y2k concerns to your doctor)*.
- Incontinence problems *(base on current use)*.
- Replacement tips and pads for crutches or walkers.
- If possible, get a spare set of dentures, eyeglasses, or hearing-aids.
- "Special" dietary items.
- Warm clothing *(extra)*.

Ensure that any equipment you depend upon has been serviced and is in good working order.

Special Needs "*Care Package*".

If you have special mobility problems or are fighting a disease or long-term illness, you will need to give careful consideration to your *"very specific needs"*.

Enlist the aid of others to help you prepare to meet these potential challenges and to develop a suitable *"care package"* that will meet your specific needs through the coming, difficult time period.

Don't forget, you have already shown great courage and strength of character in coping with your particular situation; you are more than capable of meeting these new challenges as well.

Memory Jogger for Pets.

We understand that preparing to meet your own needs and those of your family requires a lot of effort and much expense, but we also remind you that your pets too are dependent upon you for their lives.

Casey

Many people tend to think that their dogs can be turned out to fend for themselves. They cannot! The vast majority of domesticated dogs have lost the instincts necessary to survive. Dogs turned loose to fend for themselves will either be killed, die of exposure, suffer a long and painful death by starvation or will become part of feral *(wild)* packs of dogs. These dog packs are extremely dangerous to humans because they aren't afraid of us.

Cats are also dependent on their human companions to meet their needs. Although a city cat may catch an occasional bird or a mouse, their hunting skills are not adequate to keep them alive. Also, if you live in a high-rise or condo, how will your cat be able to adapt to outdoor life? Most abandoned cats die from exposure, untreated injuries, disease, or starvation.

Other pets, such as, birds, rabbits and hamsters are also completely dependent on us for their lives. They cannot survive if we fail to provide warmth, food, water and waste removal for them.

Unfortunately, it may not be easy to save reptiles and tropical fish that require carefully controlled environments which cannot be properly controlled without electricity. It is quite likely that Y2k glitches may cause electrical disruptions lasting for days or even months. Prepare for your pets and hope for the best, but be prepared for losses.

List for Pets

- Canned or pouch food.
- Cat and dog treats and also treats designed for other pets.
- Cat litter, shavings and chips for rabbits, hamsters, and mice, etc.
- Chew bones for dogs.

- Dry food *(bags)*.
- Extra medications your pet is taking for diabetes, epilepsy, heart condition, etc.
- Food for birds, fish, rabbits, rodents, reptiles and any other living thing that depends upon you.
- Medical kit or supplies for common problems such as burns, fleas, sore foot pads, etc.
- Vitamin and mineral supplements designed for your pet.
- Water — each day *(2 quarts for a medium to large size dog and 1 pint per cat or small dog)*.

Make sure your pet*(s)* has its own water bowl, food bowl, bedding and favorite toys. Also, buy and store a few new toys, bones, treats, etc., to be given at various times for reassurance and to break the monotony.

The many benefits and comforts of having your animals with you, will far outweigh any extra expense in preparing for them.

General Suggestions and Tips.

- If you are not sure how much you use of *certain* products, watch what you use in a month, then calculate what you will actually need — give yourself an *extra* margin for spills or breakage.
- Use antibacterial liquid soap *(i.e. Dial)* for sponge baths on hands, feet, privates, etc..
- Have everyone use waterless hand sanitizer *(i.e. Purell)* after going to the bathroom and before touching food, water or each other. Keeping hands free of germs is your best insurance for preventing illness.
- Bar soap *(i.e. Ivory)* is excellent for bathing, shampooing and doing hand laundry.
- Replace your tooth brush every 3 months — dip in hydrogen peroxide and rinse each day to prevent bacterial buildup.
- See your dentist for a checkup and get your most immediate dental problems fixed right away. Don't worry about the fancy or cosmetic stuff. If you have dentures or partials, have them thoroughly checked and repaired, as necessary.
- Have your eyesight checked and if you wear prescription glasses, have them updated. If you need to buy new glasses or contacts, take advantage of a two-for-one promotion and get two pairs so you have a spare.
- See your doctor and have a thorough checkup. You may want to have your inoculations updated.
- Shop for warm children's clothing and toys at *"kids-stuff only"* secondhand stores. Also, look in *"new-to-you"* shops or thrift stores for extra clothes and blankets for you and your family.
- If money is tight, have a garage or yard sale and get rid of things you don't need. Use the money you make to buy items like food, a campstove, lights and fuel.

We wish you the very best.

Self-Reliance Guidelines

Being Prepared for Anything.

Those of us who live in the city or suburbs have enjoyed a sense of confidence and security knowing that simply dialing 911 would put an emergency response team on its way to us immediately. However, most experts on the Y2k problem expect we will be unable to count on emergency services, such as: the police, fire and ambulances, or even hospital emergency rooms for *"a period of time"* after we enter into the year 2000.

If, as feared and expected, there are extensive and prolonged telephone and utility disruptions, most citizens will be on their own for a time. It is quite reasonable to expect that all emergency personnel will be kept busy with the massive and time-consuming job of responding to numerous major emergencies and attempting to maintain law and order.

We have also enjoyed and taken for granted, the *"when we want it"* availability and abundance of fully-stocked shelves at our neighborhood grocery store, pharmacy, hardware or department store. However, come January 2000 and for possibly many months after, none of these so called *"normal"* scenarios may exist. Instead, we may find shortages everywhere and in everything, and find all that we considered stable and secure — in complete chaos.

With the *"worst-case"* scenario a definite possibility *(more likely a probability)*, it is essential that YOU take full responsibility for your own well-being, safety and security by preparing to be self-reliant in the following areas:

1 Be able to provide your own heat, light, and sewage disposal.
2 Be able to prepare and cook your own food from previously stored supplies.
3 Be able to provide your own fire, home and security needs.
4 Be able to provide basic medical emergency treatment.
5 Be able to make-do and fend for yourself and your family under *"back-to-basics"* conditions.

The following guidelines have been developed to assist you in preparing to meet these various contingencies. Even though every effort has been made to make these lists as comprehensive as possible, they are also subject to conditions and legalities beyond our control or knowledge.

Since it is virtually impossible to predict what *laws* municipalities will *initiate* in the near future, we suggest that you use the following self-reliance checklists as a guideline, but be aware that you may not be in strict compliance with your local bylaws now or in the future. So use the following suggestions at your own risk.

Sewage Disposal.

In this section, we are dealing with a problem that will have enormous consequences on our well-being, our health and our environment. On a daily basis, we are reading reports indicating that we should expect major interruptions to our electricity and water supplies, due to Y2k failures.

Without electricity — we have no water; without water — our toilets won't flush. *What if they can't be used for days, weeks or even months, what will we do?* Proper disposal of human waste is necessary, if we are to prevent the contamination of our rivers and lakes and the spread of life-threatening epidemics like cholera or typhoid.

The following suggestions are listed in order of convenience and preference and will help you choose a waste disposal system you can live with for a few months:

Camping porta-potty: *(they can be emptied at any service station with a designated holding tank).* Don't forget porta-potty chemicals and deodorizers *(follow manufacturers instructions to estimate needs).*

Making do, with what you have: Place a garbage bag in your own toilet. Open it and fold it over the bowl and lower the toilet seat over the bag. Bag the results.

Portable loo: *(inexpensive to buy or to make with a toilet seat, bucket and plastic bags).* Purchase plastic bags designed for the portable loo or substitute with inexpensive, white plastic kitchen-size bags. *(Make sure they fit the unit you buy) — (get 5 boxes of 200 per person).*

Construction toilets: If your city water/sewage disposal system is off for extended periods of time, it is quite probable that the city or the military will place portable construction toilets in strategic areas, while supplies last. It is certain though, that there will be far too few of these units to meet the needs of the entire population of a large city. Our modern society may be forced to go back to the use of the family outhouse to accommodate the needs of everyone.

In a Dire Emergency.

The pit latrine: *(for 1-2 persons)* in a flat area, dig a pit about 6"- 8" deep. Cover when done.

The trench latrine: *(more than 2 persons)* dig a trench about 8" wide, 18" long and 6"- 8" deep. Straddle the pit or trench and then bury the results. Human waste will decompose in several weeks. Don't build pits near water or food sources.

Other Toiletry Needs.

- Disinfectant: Lysol or liquid bleach — *(1 bottle per month).*
- Rubber gloves: *(3-6 pairs).*
- Metal trash cans: *(Designate 1-2 for human waste and 1-2 for the disposal of diapers, sanitary napkins, or similar items).* In winter contents will freeze, in summer you may want to consider an

outhouse or a pit latrine. Be sure to dispose of bags at landfill sites well before spring thaw.
- Toilet paper *(base on current use).*
- Shovel.

Washing your hands with an antibacterial soap *(Dial)* or a waterless hand sanitizer *(Purell)* after using the bathroom and before handling food, water or touching others, will greatly reduce the risks of illness and contamination.

Alternative Cooking Sources.

Unless you want to eat cold beans or raviolli out of a can every day, you need some way of cooking the items you have stocked in your food storage pantry. In the chapter, *"Living Without Electricity"* we deal with various types of campstoves and fuel storage, so you can choose which type best fits your needs. In the midst of a dark and cold world, the sweet aroma of apple-cinnamon pancakes and coffee or nine-bean soup with skillet biscuits cooking on a campstove can make a world of difference to both your morale and health.

Basic Kitchen Equipment.

Remember, plan for no electricity. Avoid purchasing kitchen items that need electricity or recharging.

- Aluminum foil: *(2-4 rolls heavy weight foil — barbecue weight).*
- A campstove oven: *(available at most sporting or hardware stores).* These ovens work well with your campstove to make an amazing variety of tasty breads.
- Cast-iron cookware: the best, most useful type of cookware for on the campstove or camp fire, easy to clean, long lasting, and heavy. We recommend that you get a Dutch Oven with a lid, a 12-inch skillet with a lid, a flat griddle and a wok. Dutch ovens produce the best chicken and dumplings, stews, potroasts and beans you'll ever eat. They can also be used to bake bread, make cakes and cobblers. Follow the manufacturers directions for seasoning cast-iron cookware, then clean only with hot water, and towel dry. *Never use detergents.*
- Non-stick aluminum cookware set: including 2 saucepans, 1 large and 1 small or medium with lids to fit — an extra nonstick skillet is handy. *(Avoid cheap sets, as food will burn quickly if cookware is too thin).*
- Percolator coffee maker: *(buy regular grind coffee).*
- Small pressure cooker for use on portable campstove *(this is a real necessity for fuel savings, as cooking under pressure is much faster than other cooking methods).*
- Soup pot: *(medium or large size with lid) (for boiling water, making beans, pastas, or soups).*

Basic Necessities.

- Beverage holders: *(1 per person)* coffee mug, soup mug, 4 or 8 oz beverage glass.
- Cutlery: *(forks, knives, spoons)* or use plastic, disposable ones to conserve on water.
- Dishes: *(set(s) of Melamine or Corelle). (The use of paper plates can save precious water).*

Kitchen Utensils.

- Bottle opener *(1).*
- Can opener*(s) (manual, heavy-duty for reliability).*
- Ceramic bowls *(1 each, sm., med. and lge. size — better for preparing breads than glass or plastic).*
- Corkscrew *(1).*
- Funnels *(assorted sizes — use one for dry materials, one for liquids). (In a pinch, you can always make one out of aluminum foil).*
- Grater *(1).*
- Grain grinder *(manual).*
- Knives *(1 ea.) (boning, bread-loaf, butcher, carving, paring, meat or Asian cleaver, fillet).*
- Knife sharpener or whetstone.
- Matches *(paper or wooden).*
- Measuring cups *(buy a complete set each for both dry and liquid measurements; also pick up a measuring spoon set).*
- Necessary accessories: garlic press *(1)*, hot pads *(various sizes)*, large forks *(2)*, large spoons *(2-3)*, mortar and pestle for herbs *(optional)*, pancake/egg turner *(2-metal)*, plastic mixing bowls *(1 each medium and large)*, poultry scissors *(1)*, oven mitts *(1 set)*, spatula *(1)*, vegetable peeler *(2)*, wooden spoons *(different sizes).*
- Serving bowls for food.

Clean-up Items.

- Buckets for washing laundry.
- Chlorine bleach *(2-3 jugs for kitchen clean-up only).*
- Clothes line and pegs.
- Containers *(collecting/storing).*
- Dish detergent liquid *(antibacterial type) (3-4).*
- Dishpan *(1)* dish drying rack *(1).*
- Garbage can*(s)* for garbage. *(To save space, flatten boxes and cans by removing both ends and crushing underfoot. Always put trash in approved containers or take to proper dumping sites).*
- J-cloths *(to clean, soak in bleach, wash, rinse, hang to dry).*
- Liquid laundry detergent *(2-3).*
- Plastic bags *(Ziploc style freezer bags/gallon/quart size — 4 boxes of each).*
- Plastic wrap *(2-3).*
- Scouring pads *(SOS, Brillo)* and nylon scrubbers.
- Trash bags *(5 boxes (200) large/ with twist ties).*

Emergencies.

- ABC type fire extinguisher *(2) (absolutely critical! Be sure to check expiration dates).*
- Carbon monoxide detectors *(1-2) (battery operated — critical!)*
- Firearms *(both pistol and rifle are recommended; include appropriate ammunition).*
- First-aid kit *(equipped for common medical emergencies. Also, take a first-aid and CPR course, if possible).*
- Intruder alarms on doors and windows *(the type used by travellers — battery operated)* or loud dog! *(no batteries needed! just food and love).*
- Smoke detector *(battery operated only).*

First-Aid.

We suggest that everyone take a basic first-aid course including CPR training. Courses can range from a Saturday morning to a once-a-week class, lasting several weeks. Do it now, while there is still time. Later, should you find yourself forced to handle an emergency situation, your ability to cope and remain calm will be an asset to everyone around you. You won't regret it!

The following list of supplies will create an excellent first-aid kit that will cover most medical needs:

- Antibiotic cream *(2)*.
- Basic illustrated first-aid book.
- Bandages: *(type — Ace elastic) (2″ and 3″ size or 5 cm and 7.5 cm size) (1 box of each size)*.
- Bandages: sterile gauze pads, individually wrapped *(2″ x 2″ or 5 cm x 5 cm) (1 box each) (used for dressing wounds)*.
- Bandages: sterile gauze pads, individually wrapped *(3″ x 3″ or 7.5 cm x 7.5 cm)* and *(4″ x 4″ or 10 cm x 10 cm) (1 box each) (used for dressing wounds)*.
- Bandages: nonstick sterile pads *(2″ x 4″ or 4.8 cm x 7.3 cm) (used for dressing wounds) (1 box)*.
- Bandages: gauze roll *(2″ or 5 cm and 5″ or 10 cm) (used for dressing wounds) (1 roll each)*.
- Bandages: for burns *(type: Second Skin) (3″ x 3½″ or 7.5 cm by 9 cm) (1 box) (used for dressing burns)*.
- Bandages: triangular muslin, folded diagonally *(1 sq. yd or 1 sq. m.) (1 or 2) (used as a sling)*.
- *Band-Aid* type adhesive dressings: *(several boxes of various sizes and shapes, including flexible cloth-type and waterproof)*.
- Bicarbonate of soda.
- Butterfly sutures, steristrips or leukostrips *(used to hold edges of a cut or wound together)*.
- Cold/hot packs *(reusable)*.
- Cotton swabs *(1-2 boxes)* and cotton balls *(1-2 bags)*.
- Dental floss *(1-2)*.
- Epsom salts *(1 bag)*.
- Eyedropper *(1-2)*.
- First-aid tape *(1/2″ x 10 yds or 1.25 cm x 3m and 1″ x 5 yds or 2.5 cm x 5 m) (1 roll each)*.
- Gloves *(for medical and hygienic purposes) (2 packages)*.
- Hot water bottle *(1)*.
- Hydrogen peroxide *(1-2, 8 oz./ 225 ml. bottles) (use as topical antiseptic/wound cleanser)*.
- Iodine *(1)*.
- Isopropyl alcohol *(1 bottle)*.
- Meat tenderizer *(for insect bites and stings) (1)*.
- Pre-moistened towelettes *(with alcohol) (1 box)*.
- Razor blades *(single edges) (1 package)*.
- Safety pins *(assorted sizes)*.
- SAM splint *(1)*.
- Salt tablets *(1 bottle)*.
- Scalpel *(1)*.
- Scissors *(surgical pointed) (1)*.
- Thermometers *(1 oral/1 rectal)*.
- Tweezers *(1 pointed/1 flat)*.
- Water purification tablets.
- Waterless antibacterial soap.

Emergency Dental Kit.

- Dental cement.
- Dental floss.
- Gum pocket irrigator.
- Oil of cloves *(for relief of pain)*.
- Tea bags *(will control bleeding)*.
- Temporary filling mixture.
- Topical anesthetic.

Basic Handyman's Tools.

This list contains only the very basic tools you should try to have on hand. Any other tools you may already have or might acquire, will only help to make you more self-reliant.

- Axe or hatchet.
- Brace *(hand drill)*, plus a good selection of bits.
- Bubble level.
- Bungee straps *(various lengths)*.
- "C" clamps.
- Caulking gun & compound.
- Claw hammer.
- Crowbar.
- Files *(flat, hand, round, etc.)*.
- Heavy string, twine, and rope.
- Measuring tape and steel ruler.
- Nails *(assorted sizes and types)*.
- Pickaxe.
- Pliers *(combination, flat-nosed, rounded, needle-nosed, slip joint, diagonal cut, etc.)*.
- Plumbing tools *(plunger, sink waste auger)*.
- Post hole digger *(auger type — for digging holes to find water)*.
- Sandpapers and block.
- Saw file.
- Saws *(coping, crosscut, hack)*.
- Screwdrivers *(slotted, Phillips, Robertson, etc.)*.
- Screws *(assorted sizes and types)*.
- Sledge hammer.
- Staple gun and staples.
- Tape *(duct, electrical, masking)*.
- Tarps *(plastic or nylon)*.
- Vice grips *(various sizes)*.
- Winch and cable *(manual)*.
- Wire cutters.
- Wrenches *(adjustable, box, combination, crescent, monkey, pipe, multi-purpose, slip and socket)*.
- Extras: awl, square, chisels and gouges, compass, cutters for glass and tile, gauges, ladders *(extension, single, step)*, nail punches, paint brushes, planes, plumb line, propane soldering iron and torch, rasps, ratchet, snips and shears, trowels, wire strippers, etc.

Cold Weather Dressing.

The three secrets to keeping warm are layering your clothes, keeping your feet warm and preventing heat loss through the top of your head. The following wardrobe should keep you warm through the crisis.

- Arctic fleece pullovers or nylon windbreaker-type jacket lined with arctic-fleece material.
- Complete change of clothes *(3 sets per person — layered)*.
- Underwear for a week.
- Heavy winter socks or boot socks and warm slippers or moccasins will help keep your feet warm.
- Rain gear *(a rain poncho, for minimum protection, but for maximum protection each person should have a rubberized rain parka and pants. Get it oversized to allow for either warm clothes or light coat to be worn underneath)*.
- Sweat suits *(2-3 per person) (buy big so you can wear other clothing underneath)*.
- Thermal underwear — tops and bottoms *(3 per person) (A pair can be reserved as pajamas)*. Also, reserve two soft, loose, warm pairs of socks to wear inside your bed or sleeping bag and a

loose fitting cap or hood to prevent heat loss from the head while sleeping.

- Winter coat *(buy for maximum warmth and comfort, also for wind and water-resistance).*
- Winter boots treated with a waterproofing product to keep them watertight all winter. *(Buy warm, rugged, sturdy boots that offer maximum protection. No heels! Be fashionably unfashionable!) (2 pairs in case one gets wet).*
- Don't forget these items: a balaklava or toque, gloves, hats, two pairs of heavy duty work gloves, mittens, scarves, extra sweaters, windbreakers, etc.

Identification and Documents.

Obtain hard copies of: adoption, birth, marriage and divorce decrees, and death certificates; automobile, home, fire and life insurance policies; passports or visas, social security/insurance numbers *(including statement on earnings and benefits)*; court orders; contracts, deeds and wills; records from any personal or business bank accounts, credit card account numbers and their "lost or stolen" notification numbers or addresses, stocks, bonds and mutual funds *(get brokerage records)*, RRSP's, GIC's, RIF's; pension or retirement records, military service records; copies of your most recent electrical, water, gas and telephone bill payments, current records of tax and mortgage payments; medical records *(include any immunization records)*, medical, dental or drug plan identification; inventory of household items; pet records and immunizations.

Put these items in a waterproof container and store them where they will be safe but can be accessed quickly. Keep originals in another safe location. Lastly, keep an up-to-date address book of friends and family.

Miscellaneous.

- ***Arts and craft supplies:*** Stock-up on crayons, colored pencils and pens, coloring books, construction paper, drawing paper, glue, paints, and some simple craft supplies for entertaining and keeping children busy and occupied without TV.
- ***Bibles:*** Get several different versions such as, *The New Living Translation, Amplified Version, New King James, and New International Version*. They will provide variety in your reading, help you understand the Bible better and provide you and your family with hope and comfort.
- ***Books:*** Two important books you should have in your library are: *(1)* a first-aid manual and *(2)* a camping and wilderness survival manual. Make sure they have good illustrations and explanations — either could save your life! Keep both of these books close at hand, so you can quickly grab them in an emergency and go.
- Also, we suggest you buy a few gardening and back-to-basics homesteading books that ex-

plain how to raise your own food and preserve it, raise animals for food or barter, etc. However, make your selections carefully as most back-to-basics or homesteading books *assume* you are in a *rural setting* and are already equipped for the *rigors* of rural life.

- Also, prepare for your children to continue their education at home. Without electricity or water, schools will not be open, except perhaps as shelters. Since all available resources will be used to get the utilities up and running, children may be out of school for several weeks or months. Stockpile books that will help your children continue their education. There are many "tutoring" books available on various subjects, such as: grammar, math, science, etc., for different ages and grade needs. You may want to add to your home library some educational books — full of illustrations and useful information, illustrated history books, a variety of classic literature, poetry, and a fairly recent encyclopedia, such as World Book which is good for young readers to adults. *(buy from used book stores and/or yard sales).*
- Put aside a variety of unread books for yourself and other family members. *(Consider boredom an enemy; it dulls the mind and opens the door to frustration and depression).*
- ***Bicycles for each person:*** Aside from walking, it may be your only form of transportation. Make sure you have at least one good, strong carrying basket mounted on each bike. Also, have a few hand tools, a hand pump and a tire repair kit available for roadside repairs.
- ***Buttons:*** Assorted sizes.
- ***Canning and home preserving equipment:*** Get a big pot with a lid or a pressure cooker, timer, mason jars, etc.
- ***Clock:*** Windup or travel style.
- ***Games:*** Board games, card and tile games *(i.e. Scrabble, Checkers, Dominos, Chess, etc.).*
- ***Homes:*** Make sure your home is well insulated, and that the roof doesn't leak — seal all drafts. If you have a fireplace or wood stove make sure it is clean, in good repair and that you have enough wood.
- ***Needles and thread:*** Assorted sizes and colors and weights.
- ***Office supplies:*** Erasers, glue sticks, journals, magnifying glass, notebooks, paper, paper clips, pencils *(plain and colored),* manual pencil sharpener, pens *(various colored inks),* rubber bands, scotch-tape dispenser and refills, stapler and refills, etc.
- ***Pins:*** Straight *(1 box)*; safety pins - *(1 box assorted sizes).*
- ***Radio:*** Battery operated or solar powered. Tune it to the Emergency Broadcast Channel in your area. Listen only for a short period each day; don't drain your batteries. Keep some extra batteries on hand.
- ***Stockpile:*** Anything you think

you may need for your family, home, or survival. Your main concerns will be water, food, shelter, warmth, hygiene and protection for you and your family.

- ***Toys:*** Put aside a few new toys, games, or small stuffed animals to be brought out during those *"difficult"* times.
- ***Yarn:*** *(Stockpile enough for knitting or crocheting projects).*

Self-Reliance Skills.

Learn to knit or crochet simple hats, mitts, slippers, sweaters, vests; learn basic sewing stitches for repair; learn how to make your own soap and candles; learn basic wiring and plumbing, etc.; take a first-aid and CPR course; take any *"outdoor courses"* offered in your area that will teach you basic survival skills, help you identify edible and dangerous plants, find water, and navigate by compass and map.

Always err on the side of putting away too much. Extra food, fuel or other supplies can always be bartered, shared or given away to others, but having too little puts you and your family at risk. Also, items will cost much more when stocks become severely limited.

Preparing for the Worst.

This section deals with the *"absolute worst-case scenario."* If your conditions get so bad that you and your family are forced into a camping-type or transient survival situation, the only way you can guarantee your safety *THEN*, is to be as fully prepared as possible *NOW!*

This type of survival situation is very serious and requires careful thought and planning. If you must leave the city, plan exactly where you are going, how long it will take to get there, what you need for your journey and what you need when you arrive. Make sure that when you arrive, your destination will provide you and your family with shelter, water, food and safety. Note: Everyone's needs are different. The following list provides suggestions from which to build your own survival packs. Only purchase items that give you the maximum ability to be self-reliant at the lightest weight. Remember, your survival may be based on what you can carry!

A good rule-of-thumb is that you can carry one-fifth *(easily)* to one-fourth *(harder)*, your own body weight on your back. For example: a 200 lb man can easily carry a 35-50 lb pack and a child of 60 lbs can easily carry a 12-15 lb pack. Each person in the family *(including children and even the dog)* should have a backpack equipped specifically for them to distribute the necessary gear evenly. Choose the items that most suit your needs.

- Axe or hatchet.
- Baby carrier *(if applicable).*
- Backpack *(external frame).*
- Campstove *(backpacker-style including fuel cartridges).*
- Candles *(emergency/long life).*

- Can opener.
- Canteen*(s)* — for water.
- Change of clothes / underwear.
- Compass and maps.
- Cooking tools.
- Dish washing liquids.
- Dog pack: leash, collar, food, water, bowl and current dog tags.
- Don't forget: important personal papers, plastic tubing, razor blades, scissors, string, tin can for candle, etc. *(Study outdoor survival lists for other items).*
- Fire grill.
- Fire starters.
- First-aid kit *(compact).*
- Fishing kit *(emergency type).*
- Flashlight *(get extra batteries and bulb).*
- Folding camp chairs *(small, lightweight and comfortable).*
- Folding drinking cup.
- Folding saw *(wood for fire).*
- Food *(broth cubes, chocolate bars, dehydrated and freeze-dried foods, dried fruits, granola bars, hard candies, nuts, instant soups, hot chocolate or tea packages).*
- Garbage bags.
- Ground cloth.
- Inflatable pillow.
- Insect repellent.
- Lantern *(backpacker-style using same fuel as cook-stove).*
- Light sticks *(chemical).*
- Lighter *(butane).*
- Mosquito netting.
- Nesting aluminum cookware *(backpacker-style).*
- Nesting type dinnerware *(backpacker style for portability).*
- Nesting utensil kit.
- Nylon cord.
- Personal items: *(aspirin, biodegradable bar soap, dental floss, diarrhea medication, foot and nail care items, liquid washing soap, shampoo, toothbrush, toothpaste, towel, etc.).*
- Plastic sheeting or tarpaulin.
- Plastic bags *(re-sealable).*
- Portable clothes line with pegs.
- Prescriptions or medications.
- Rain poncho or rain gear
- Sewing kit *(compact).*
- Sharpening stone.
- Shovel.
- Signal equipment *(flares, mirror).*
- Sleeping bag *(lightweight but warm)* with sleeping pad.
- Snake bite kit.
- Snaring kit *(wire).*
- Soap *(1 bar for each person).*
- Space blankets.
- Sunglasses and sunblock.
- Survival manual.
- Swiss army knife *(each person).*
- Tent and/or pup-tent for kids *(plus pegs, poles and mallet).*
- Tent repair kit.
- Toilet items.
- Towels.
- Vitamin/mineral supplements.
- Warm weather travel items.
- Wash basin *(inflatable).*
- Water jug *(collapsible).*
- Water purification tablets.
- Waterproof matches.
- Whistle *(one for each person).*

Please note: this list cannot be considered comprehensive due to individual needs and requirements, but it should provide a foundational guide for getting started.

Ten Common Food-Storage Mistakes

Starting Out Right!
Before you begin your Y2k food storage shopping program, please read the following article. It has been developed to help you avoid making serious, potentially life-threatening mistakes.

Failure to Plan: One of the most serious mistakes you can make is to go out in a panic and buy everything in sight you think you'll need. This is where you can make many serious buying mistakes. You'll find yourself with items you may not be able to use because key ingredients are missing, or you'll have items with too short a shelf-life or items with poor nutritional quality *(junk food)*. You might even pick up items that need to be cooked in appliances that may no longer work.

Stockpiling the Wrong Items: It is almost a certainty that many parts of the country, even the world, will experience electrical interruptions or be without electricity for lengthy periods of time. How long these outages may be is unknown. For this reason, it is vitally important that you ***do not*** plan your food storage shopping program around your freezer, refrigerator, stove or microwave. Without electricity, all the food in your refrigerator and freezer will spoil in a few days and your electric appliances will be useless. Buy a camping or backpacking stove, and plan meals that can be easily prepared in a Dutch oven or fry pan. Camping ovens are available, which will allow you to make quality bread, casseroles or muffins. Don't plan meals that require eggs, milk, fresh food or other refrigerated items as these may not be available.

All your eggs in one basket: Many people are being lured into buying *"survival packages"* from companies that advertise *"complete packages"* containing a full year's supply of food. Many of these companies are legitimate, but most are operating 6-9 months behind schedule and aren't able to meet current demands. As the Y2k deadline draws nearer, how can new customer orders arrive in time? Also, some outfits are sending out orders that contain poor quality food items and far less than a year's worth. If you want to buy from these companies do so; however, you would be wiser to start today and stockpile canned and dry items from your local grocery store, to make sure you have enough food on your shelves. Get your food in place well before January 1, 2000 to avoid shortages, high prices and certain runs on grocery stores.

One Item Buying: Each time you shop you should buy a variety of foods to put aside. It is dangerous to follow certain suggested buying programs based on buying only one particular item each week.

Those programs may be good during normal times, but we are no longer living in normal times. If, for any number of reasons, a run happens on the grocery store, you must protect your family by making sure you are putting away a ***variety*** of foods and items that will allow you to eat for at least a few months.

No Variety: Many are following a suggested list that recommends storing four food items — wheat, milk, honey, salt. Although this could provide you with bread *(if you can bake it)*, you'll be sick of it within a day, much less having to depend on it *as your sole source of food* for a full 6-12 months. Variety is the most important thing for you to consider in your food storage pantry. Follow the "*Choices*" list, add some freeze-dried foods if you like, some no-cook items and anything else that will break the monotony of Y2k shortages.

Trying to Be Something You're Not: The crisis produced by Y2k will, in itself, be stressful enough without having to make a complete lifestyle change at midnight. If you've lived exclusively on fast food or microwave dinners, you're not suddenly going to become an all-natural cook overnight. However, your very life and survival will depend on what items you store, the nutritional value it contains and your ability to cook it. From the "*Choices*" guide, buy foods you like and learn *NOW* how to make some new foods from scratch.

Being Afraid to Try New Foods: Buying and cooking new types of foods, such as dried beans or grains can be intimidating but they are actually very easy to prepare, give you lots of variety, and taste good as well. Stock-up! The "*Back to Basics Cookery*" section will give you basic foolproof guidelines for preparing these new foods.

Forgetting Water: Just about all of the most nutritious foods require water for preparation, *(beans, rice, pastas, sprouts, etc.)* We recommend storing a minimum of one gallon of water, per person, per day. This should cover all your cooking needs. However, you will never be sorry if you decide to store some extra water just for cooking or whatever.

Storing Incorrectly: It costs a lot of money to store enough food and water for a six month period — make sure your storage area is the best it can be. Store all food items in a cool *(35°- 65°F)*, dry, dark, well-ventilated area. Make sure items can't freeze, get wet, or attacked by insects or rodents. Date everything and put most recently purchased items at the back. Use the items from the front of the shelf first.

The worst mistake of all
is
leaving it until it's too late!

Food Storage - What Are Your Choices?

Prepare Now!

Nothing will give you more peace of mind than opening a cupboard door and seeing it full of stored foods. Each can, bottle and package becomes an investment for yourself and your family, from which you can draw when needed. They represent your preparedness, your self-reliance and your future.

Although there are many excellent companies that produce survival packages, dehydrated foods and M.R.E's, many of these companies are already, *(a year before the crisis)*, overwhelmed by the huge demand for their packages and many are presently experiencing delays of six months or longer in processing customer orders. Some companies are now beginning to admit that they may be unable to fulfill *existing orders* in time — if at all.

Buying ***your own supplies*** from your local supermarket allows you to be in full control. Every day or week you can add to your survival cupboard, items you and your family like and that store well. This allows you to know how well prepared you are and eliminates the fear of not being ready should runs begin on the grocery stores.

Optimum Storage Conditions.

Storing foods in cool, dry cabinets or on shelves in a room with a ***constant*** temperature of 40°- 50°F with a relative humidity level of 50-60% would be ideal. Digital gauges that display both *temperature and humidity levels* are available at most hardware and department stores.

Storage temperature should never go below 35°F or above 70°F. If the storage area is too cold, foods can freeze and your supplies will be destroyed in a few hours; if it is too warm the nutritional quality of the food deteriorates very quickly. If there is too much moisture, dry goods can develop molds or rust can form on cans. Items in glass jars should be stored in a dark area as light hastens deterioration. Cooler temperatures also tend to inhibit insect infestations.

Shelf-life.

Most canned foods, foods in jars and many packaged staples have a relatively long shelf-life. By using proper storage conditions, many of these foods will retain their nutritional value far longer than recommended storage times.

When putting new food items away, mark the date on it with a permanent marker, then store it *behind* any existing stock. This practice is called rotation. It ensures that you use older food first.

Suggestions and Tips.

- Buy from a store with a quick turnover. Never buy dusty cans *(indicates old stock)* or dented ones. Avoid rusty cans.

- Buy items your family likes, but make sure you store a variety of foods to break the monotony. Even a favorite food loses it's appeal when eaten too often.
- Add to your food pantry items that may be new to you — grains, lentils, or dried beans. Many of these foods are quite nutritious; you may actually eat better *during this crisis* than now.
- Always buy the *best quality* foods that you can.
- Buy *low-sodium* varieties whenever possible.
- Combine your buying efforts with others and save money on bulk quantities.
- You have nothing to lose and everything to gain by storing food. *If nothing happens*, thank God and give the extra food to your local food bank. *If something does happen*, thank God and enjoy the food you have put away.

Caution.

Some products must be refrigerated after opening. If electricity is sporadic, food spoilage becomes a serious issue. If you live in a cold area, you may be able to store some items requiring refrigeration outside in coolers, but keep items from freezing. *Refrigeration temperatures is considered 35°- 40°F and frozen foods must be kept under 32°F consistently.* To be safe though, buy products that require refrigeration *(ketchup, mayo, mustard, jams, etc.)* in the smallest-sized containers you can or in restaurant-size packages that require no refrigeration.

Being Prepared.

The following list was developed to provide you with the maximum amount of choices for your food storage cupboard. The list shows:

- the optimum shelf-life
- best storage conditions
- special handling requirements
- choices available.

Note: In some lists you will see two numbers — the first indicates the shelf-life of the item *unopened*, the second number following the slash *(/)* indicates the shelf-life after *opening*. The abbreviation r.a.o. means *refrigerate after opening*, u.b.e.d. means *use by expiration date* on package, and f.g. means *food grade*. If a product has a *(+)* symbol after it, it will keep indefinitely.

Baby Food.

- dry food products *(12 months)*, canned or glass *(12 months)*, formulas *(12 months or u.b.e.d.)*
- store in a cool, dry place
- keep glass jars and liquids in a cool, dry, dark place

Baby-to-toddler meals, biscuits, cereals, juices, nursing formula, pabulum, puréed fruits and vegetables.

Beans *(canned)*.

- 24 months
- store in a cool, dry place
- unless the sauce is intended to add flavor to the beans *(i.e. chili)*, drain the canning fluids away and rinse well. These fluids will cause flatulence.

Miscellaneous beans, beans in molasses or tomato sauce, chili's, refried beans, salad mixes, soups.

Beans *(dried).*

- 12 months
- store in a cool, dry place
- airtight/moistureproof – glass, metal or f.g. plastic containers
- see *Back to Basics Cookery* for more detailed information

Adzuki, black bean, black-eyed bean, black kidney bean, borlotti bean, broad bean, brown bean, cannellini bean *(Great Northern),* **chickpea** *(garbanzo),* **haricot bean, lentil, lima bean, mixed bean soup mixes, mung bean, navy, pinto, red kidney, soybean.**

Baking Ingredients.

- 12–24 months *(average).* Some last indefinitely; others u.b.e.d.
- store in a cool, dry place
- airtight/moistureproof – glass, metal or f.g. plastic containers
- keep liquid extracts in the dark

Baking powder *(18/6m),* **baking soda** *(24/6m),* **cornstarch** *(+),* **cream of tarter** *(+),* **dry yeast** *(u.b.e.d.),* **flavored extracts** *(rum, almond 24/12m),* **gelatin** *(18m),* **real vanilla extract** *(24/12m).*

Beverages.

- 18–36 months *(average)*
- store in a cool, dry place
- make water your ***first*** choice

Coffee-*instant (12m/4w),* **coffee**-*percolator and drip grinds (12m/4w),* **fruit drinks**-*powdered (18m),* **fruit juice**-*canned/tetra pak (24m),* **Gator Aide** *(18m),* **instant hot cocoa** *(8m),* **Kool-Aid** *(18m),* **meal replacement drinks** *(12m/u.b.e.d),* **Tang** *(18m),* **tea**-*herbal (18m),* **tea**-*regular (36m),* **vegetable juice**-*canned/tetra pak (24m).*

Breakfast Products.

- store in a cool, dry place
- airtight/moistureproof – glass, metal or f.g. plastic containers

Fruit bars *(3-6m),* **granola bars** *(3-6m),* **pancake mixes** – *complete, just add water (9-12m).*

Cereals.

- ready-to-eat *(12m unopened/2-3m opened),* cereals–*cooked (6m)*
- store in a cool, dry place
- airtight/moistureproof – glass, metal or f.g. plastic containers

Cold breakfast cereals *(corn, oat, rice, wheat),* **granola types, hot breakfast cereals,** *(cream of wheat and similar types),* **oatmeal** *(instant), (rolled 18m),* **"O" type cereals** *(Cheerios).*

Chocolate /Chocolate Substitutes.

- keep chocolate cool and tightly wrapped, but not cold
- dark chocolate lasts for years if stored properly but milk and white chocolate last only about 9 months
- cocoa should be stored in an air-tight, moistureproof container, in a cool, dark place
- carob *(a chocolate substitute)* will keep indefinitely in an airtight container, in a cool place

Carob *(chips, chunks, powder) (+),* **cocoa powder** *(24m),* **chocolate semisweet** *(24m),* **unsweetened** *(18m),* **chocolate chips** *(24m),* **chocolate syrup** *(24m/12m+ r.a.o).*

Comfort Foods.

- choose items that you and your family really like, enjoy and consider as special treats. Everyone can handle a difficult situation *better* when they can still enjoy *"a little treat"*— even in the middle of the worst circumstances. Most *"treats"* last for 12 months. Don't buy and store a lot of junk foods!

Banana chips *(8m)*, **butterscotch candies** *(+)*, **caramels, chewing gum, fruit leathers, hard candies** *(+)*, **M&M's, popcorn** *(36m jar or can/bag 3m)*, **sesame seed/honey bars, toffee, trail mix, vacuum packed peanuts** *(24m)*.

Crackers or Bread Products.

- store in a cool, dry place
- airtight/moistureproof – glass, metal or f.g. plastic containers

Bread crumbs *(6m)*, **Holland rusks** *(12m)*, **melba toast** *(12m)*, **pretzels** *(3m)*, **Ritz/Saltines** *(8m)*.

Dried and Packet Foods.

- store in a cool, dry place
- airtight/moistureproof – glass, metal or plastic containers

Bouillon cubes and powders *(chicken, beef, and vegetable - 24m)*, **cup-a-soup mixes** *(24m)*, **dry soup packets** *(12m)*, **instant bases for sauces or gravies** *(12-24m)*, **powdered eggs** *(36m)*, **dry dessert topping** *(12m)*.

Dried Fruits.

- 12–18 months
- store in a cool, dry place
- airtight/moistureproof – glass, metal or plastic containers

Apple, apricot, cherries, cranberries, citrus peels, currants, dates, figs, nectarines, peaches, pears, prunes, raisins.

Dried *(dehydrated)* Vegetables.

- 12–18 months
- store in a cool, dry place
- original foil packages or airtight/moistureproof – glass, metal or plastic containers

Celery, chili peppers, mushrooms, onions, peas, peppers, potatoes, sun-dried tomatoes, vegetable flakes.

Extracts *(chicken, beef, vegetable)*.

- 24 months
- store in a cool, dry place
- airtight/moistureproof – glass, metal or plastic containers
- keep bottled extracts in the dark
- buy low-sodium types

Bovril, bouillon cubes and powders, canned broths, consommés.

Fats and Oils.

- most are good for 8-12 months
- store in a cool, dry place
- store glass bottles in a dark place *(light speeds deterioration)*

Butter flavored and regular shortening, canola, ghee, lard, olive oil, peanut, sesame, safflower, soy, sunflower, vegetable shortening.

Fish *(canned)*.

- 18 months
- store in a cool, dry place

Anchovy, clams, crab, herrings, kippers, mackerel, mussels, oysters, salmon, sardines, shrimp, tuna.

Flours.

- 6-12 months *(white flours 12m, whole grains 6m, tortilla flour 6m)*
- store in a cool, dry place
- airtight/moistureproof – glass,

metal or f.g. plastic containers

- see *Back to Basics Cookery* for more detailed information

All-purpose, barley, bread, bran, cake, corn, cornmeal, gluten, malt, oat, oat-bran, pastry, rice, rye, self-rising, soya, triticale, white, wholegrains, whole-wheat.

Fruits *(canned or glass).*

- 24 months *(any style — sliced, halved, sauced or whole)*
- store in a cool, dry place

Applesauce, berries, cherries, fruit cocktail, mango, papaya, peaches, pears, pineapples.

Fruit Juices *(canned or tetra pak).*

- 24 months *(100% fruit or nectars are best)*
- store in a cool, dry place

Apple, apricot, mango, mixed fruits, orange juice and blends, papaya, peach, pear, pineapple, include vegetable blends.

Grains.

- 6–12 months
- store in a cool, dry, dark place
- airtight/moistureproof – glass, metal or plastic containers
- see *Back to Basics Cookery* for more detailed information

Amaranth *(whole grain, popped, flour)*, **barley** *(pot, scotch, pearl, flakes, flour)*, **bran** *(oat, wheat)*, **buckwheat** *(seeds, groats, flour)*, **bulgur, corn** *(meal, flour)*, **hominy** *(grits)*, **couscous, matzo meal, millet, oats** *(flakes, flour)*, **oatmeal** *(flakes, flour, groats, rolled, steel-cut)*, **polenta, quinoa, rye** *(flakes, flour, cracked)*, **wheat** *(berries, cracked, germ, rolled wheat flakes)*.

Heat-and-Serve Meals *(canned).*

- 24 months
- store in a cool, dry place

Chili, chili-con-carne, pasta and sauce meals, stews, etc.

Herbs *(dried).*

- 12–24 months
- store in a cool, dry, dark place
- use airtight glass jars

Basil, bay leaves, dill, fennel, Italian herb seasoning, oregano, parsley, pepper ground, rosemary, sage, savory, tarragon, thyme.

Honey.

- 12 months for liquid honey, 6 months for comb-type
- store in a cool, dry, dark place
- in airtight containers

Comb, chunk, creamed, liquid, spun. Use restaurant size packages, for quick energy treats.

Jams and Jellies.

- 18 mo. *(unopened)*, 3 mo. *(r.a.o.)*
- store in a cool, dry place

Whenever possible, buy a few restaurant-size packages of your favorites. Use within one day, if you are unable to refrigerate.

Lentils and Split Peas.

- 12 months
- store in a cool, dry place
- airtight/moistureproof – glass, metal or plastic containers

Brown, green, red lentils; dried green peas, split green or yellow peas.

Meat *(canned).*

- 12 months
- store in a cool, dry place

There are many different types and styles of canned meat products — try to get a good variety.
Chicken, corned beef, ham, patés, Spam types, tinned luncheon meats *(chicken, ham, turkey)*, etc.

Milk and Milk Substitutes.

- tetra-pak ***real milk*** *(6 months)*, canned milk *(12 months or u.b.e.d.)*, dry powdered milk *(12 months or u.b.e.d.)*
- store in a cool, dry place
- airtight/moistureproof – glass, metal or f.g. plastic containers
- make only small amounts of reconstituted dried milk as it must be kept cold after mixing. Transfer leftover canned milk to a covered container and chill. *(Both last for 2 days at 30°- 40°F)*

Condensed or concentrated skim and whole milk, evaporated skim and whole milk, powdered dry milk, sweetened condensed milk (6m). *Note:* You cannot substitute sweetened, condensed milk for condensed or evaporated milk.

Mustards.

- 12 months for mustard seed and dry ground mustard
- 24 months *(unopened)* prepared mustards, indefinitely if kept cold *(30°- 40°F)*. Use in 1-2 day otherwise.
- store in cool, dry, dark place

American, Chinese, Dijon, dry, English, German, Russian-styles, coarse or whole grain.

Noodles *(dried)*.

- 24 months *(indefinitely when stored properly)*
- store in cool, dry place
- airtight/moistureproof – glass, metal or f.g. plastic containers
- dried noodles, made from bean-starch, buckwheat, egg, rice, or wheat, are readily available in the International section of most supermarkets or Asian shops.

Cellophane, egg, Ramen, Shanghai, soba, and udon are the most commonly used noodles. *(There are so many types of noodles to choose from — experiment to discover the ones you like most and store these).*

Nuts, Seeds and Peanut Butter.

- due to their high fat content, nuts and seeds can go rancid quickly. To help prevent this, store all nuts and seeds in airtight containers away from light, heat and moisture. Store in a cool, dark, dry place.
- shelled nuts can be kept cold in an airtight container for up to 4 months or frozen for up to 8 months. *(As a general rule, depending on their freshness at the time of storage, unshelled nuts will keep twice as long as shelled).*
- vacuum-packed tinned nuts are good for 24 months
- a rancid product can be identified by an offensive, rank smell and taste. *Do not eat!*.
- Peanut butter with preservatives will keep *indefinitely* in a cool place. Natural peanut butter must be kept cold *(6m)*

Nuts: almond, Brazil, cashew, hazelnut, macadamia, peanut, pecan, pistachio and walnut. Seeds: caraway, poppy, sesame and sunflower seeds.

Pasta and Pasta Sauces.

- 24 months+
- store in cool, dry place
- airtight/moistureproof – glass, metal or f.g. plastic containers
- buy brands made with durum wheat *(also called semolina)*
- varieties include egg pastas, grain and whole meal pastas, herb and vegetable pastas.
- see *Back to Basics Cookery* for more detailed information
- choose pastas that go well with prepared tomato-based sauces. Buy a large selection of pasta sauces which will allow you to enjoy a delicious variety of tastes, even if you manage to store only one type of pasta.
- Since refrigeration may be a problem, experiment with recipes that don't rely on fresh eggs, milk, meat, cheese or vegetables in their preparation, as these products may not be available for many months.

Angel-hair, elbow macaroni, farfalle, fettuccine, fusilli, lasagne, penné, rigatoni, rotelle, shells and spaghetti are some of the most commonly used pastas. Store canned versions of **spaghetti, ravioli, etc.** for quick heat-and-serve meals.

Pet Food.

- 18 months
- store in cool, dry place
- airtight/moistureproof – glass, metal or f.g. plastic containers

Canned, dried or foil packaged food for dogs, cats, birds and any other living thing for which you are the caregiver.

Rice.

- white rice can be stored for 12 to 24 months. Brown rice, however, can only be stored for 6 months as it is highly susceptible to rancidity. For longer storage, chill or freeze.
- store in a cool, dry place
- airtight/moistureproof – glass, metal or f.g. plastic containers
- see *Back to Basics Cookery* for more detailed information

Arborio, basmati, brown, converted, instant, jasmine, risotto, Thai rice, white, wild.

Salt and Seasonings.

- 24 months+
- any type of salt or high-salt content items will last indefinitely.
- store in cool, dry, dark place

Black pepper or peppercorns *(48m)*, Cajun, garlic cloves *(6m)* garlic salt, lemon pepper, *Mrs. Dash.*

Snacks.

- 12 months *(hard biscuit-types)*
- store in cool, dry place
- airtight/moistureproof – glass, metal or f.g. plastic containers

Bagel chips, cookies *(arrowroot, chocolate chip, gingersnaps, oatmeal, social tea or similar)*, **cake and muffin mixes** *(add water only-8m)*, **ready-to-eat puddings or fruit cups** *(12m)*, **vanilla wafers** *(6m)*. *Pick your favorites.*

Soups *(canned)*.

- 24 months
- store in cool, dry place
- purchase heat-and-serve types of soups whenever possible

Bean soups, beef noodle, chicken noodle, chunky, clam chowder, lentil, minestrone, mushroom, onion, pea, tomato, vegetable. Stock some **broths, cheddar and creamy soups.**

Spices *(ground or whole).*

- 24 months
- store in cool, dry, dark place

Allspice, caraway, cardamon, chili powder and flakes, cinnamon, cloves, coriander, cumin, curry powder, garlic minced and powder, ginger, meat tenderizer, nutmeg, paprika, poultry seasoning, tumeric.

Sprouting Seeds and Beans.

- store in cool, dry, dark place
- glass containers are best
- buy organic seeds from a health food store, mail order supplier or from a speciality shop.

Adzuki*, alfalfa*, chick-pea, clover, fenugreek, garlic, lentils*, mung beans*, onion, radish, soybean and sweet pea are the most popular to grow. Also try **barley, oats, rye and wheat.** *(* indicates best seeds or beans to stock.)*

Sugars.

- indefinitely – if stored properly
- store in cool, dry, dark place
- airtight/moistureproof – glass, metal or plastic containers

Brown, cane, cubed or granulated white, icing sugar, sugar substitutes, turbinado.

Supplements.

- 24 months
- store in cool dry, dark place

With potential shortages of fresh fruits and vegetables an almost certainty, it would be very wise to plan on adding supplements to your food storage cupboard. Consider getting a multivitamin/ mineral supplement, additional calcium, vitamins E and C and an immune system booster such as echinacea.

Syrups and Sweeteners.

- store in cool dry, dark place

Corn syrup - light and dark *(12m)*, **"golden" syrup, pure maple syrup** *(6m)*, **honey** *(8m)*, **molasses** *(12m)*, **artificial sweeteners** *(24m)*.

Tomato Products *(canned/ jars).*

- most canned or bottled tomato products last 24 months
- store in cool, dry place and dark if storing items in clear glass

Crushed, diced, paste, sauce, stewed, whole. Include specialty varieties like Italian or Mexican styles. Stock a *wide variety* of pasta sauces.

Vegetables *(canned/jars).*

- 24 months
- store in cool, dry place

Artichokes, asparagus, beets, carrots, corn, creamed corn, green or yellow beans, mixed vegetables, mushrooms, peas, potatoes, sauerkraut, spinach, yams, etc.

Vinegars.

- 24 months+
- store in cool, dry, dark place

Balsamic, cider, distilled or white, herb flavored, malt, rice, wine.

Back to Basics Cookery

BEANS.

Beans have been called the *"near-perfect food"*. They are high in complex carbohydrates, protein, dietary fiber, low in fat and sodium and have no cholesterol. They are a superior source of B vitamins, iron, calcium and potassium.

They have been called *"the meat that grows on vines"* because of their high protein levels *(20-40%)*. They are the best source of non-meat protein available. However, the protein is incomplete, lacking the amino acid methionine. To make beans a complete protein, simply add rice or a pasta side dish, bread, tortilla, or meat.

Bite-for-bite, beans provide the best nutrition of any long-term storage staple you can put away.

Selecting and Storing Beans.

Choose beans that are plump, clean, smooth and have a satiny sheen. Avoid buying packages which contain beans that are dull, discolored, cracked, shriveled, or have tiny holes which indicate bugs. Beans will keep indefinitely if frozen, or for a full year when stored in airtight containers in a cool, dry place. Always try to buy the freshest packages possible as beans that are old will not cook properly.

Bean Math.

- 1 lb *(500mg)* dried beans = 2- 2½ cups *(500-625 mL)* uncooked = 5-6 cups *(1.25-1.5L)* cooked
- 1 cup *(500 mL)* dried beans = 2-2½ cups *(500-625 mL)* cooked
- 1 Can *(19 oz/540 mL)* beans = 1½ cups *(375 mL)* drained beans

Preparing Dried Beans.

- Sort through the beans and discard any damaged beans, tiny twigs, leaves or stones, then thoroughly rinse to make sure they are clean.
- Beans must be soaked before cooking to gradually replace the water lost during drying, to speed up cooking time and to remove some of the substances that cause gas in humans.
- **Slow Soak:** soak beans in cool water that is 3 times their volume *(1 cup beans = 3 cups water)*, for 6-8 hours or overnight. In warm weather, beans can go sour if left to soak too long before cooking.
- **Quick Soak:** Cover beans with about 3 cups of water, then bring to a boil for 2-3 minutes. Remove from heat and let stand for 1 hour.
- Discard the water the beans soaked in from either of the soaking methods and rinse the beans. Do not use this water for drinking or cooking purposes, as it will cause flatulence. Cover beans with fresh water and cook as recommended.

- Dried peas and lentils should not be presoaked. Always wash them thoroughly before using, to remove dust or debris. Black-eyed or yellow-eyed peas and chick-peas ***are beans*** and are, therefore, presoaked.

Cooking Beans.

- Cook beans in a large, heavy saucepan. Beans swell to several times their dry size during cooking and you risk boil-overs if your pot is too small.
- Cover the beans with water *(1 cup beans to 3 cups water)*. Bring them to a boil for several minutes. This is important as beans contain a toxin called lectin, which can cause stomach cramps, nausea or diarrhea, if beans are undercooked when eaten. Serve when tender.
- After boiling several minutes, reduce the heat and **simmer** the beans uncovered for 1 to 3 hours depending on the type of bean. Stir them occasionally. Skim off any scum that rises to the top and discard. Add hot water if necessary. Beans should always be completely covered.
- Split peas and lentils cook faster, taking only about 30 minutes to an hour to fully cook.
- To test for doneness, remove a few beans from the pot. They should mash easily between your fingers, but not be mushy.
- Beans can be cooked quickly in a pressure cooker. This can help conserve precious fuel if you are using a campstove. Follow the manufacturers directions.

Bean Cooking Secrets.

- Always simmer dried beans as prolonged boiling can cause the pot to boil over, the beans to break apart and the skins to separate.
- Add 2-3 teaspoons vegetable oil to the water to prevent foaming and boil-overs when cooking.
- Cook beans uncovered if you want firm-textured beans or covered if you want them soft.
- Do not add salt to soaking or cooking water. It will inhibit the beans from absorbing liquid and make them tough. Add salt only during the last 10 to 15 minutes of cooking or when served.
- Don't add acidic foods such as tomatoes to beans during cooking because doing so will cause them to toughen or split. Wait until beans are thoroughly cooked, then add and heat.
- Do not combine beans that need different cooking times. It is best to cook them separately and then combine when done. If you want a variety of beans, carefully time their introduction to the pot — add those needing the longest cooking times first.
- Add dense vegetables like carrots or turnips early so that they have time to become tender. Add tender vegetables like onions or peppers in the middle or near the end for best flavor.
- Add dried seasoning halfway through cooking time to allow them to release all their flavors. Add delicate, fresh herbs when the beans are almost done.

Bean Types and Varieties					
Type of Bean	Soak Time	Simmer Time	Simmer Water Needed	Pressure Cooker Time	1 Cup of Dry Beans Yields
Black Bean	Overnight	1-1½ hrs.	3 cups	10-15 min.	2¼ cups
Black-eyed Peas	Overnight	1-1½ hrs.	3 cups	10 min.	2 cups
Cannellini	Overnight	1½-2 hrs.	3 cups	20 min.	2 cups
Chick-peas	Overnight	1½-2 hrs.	3-4 cups	No	2¼ cups
Cranberry	Overnight	1½-2 hrs.	3 cups	15-20 min.	2 cups
Fava (Broad)	Overnight	2-2½ hrs.	4 cups	No	2 cups
Flageolet	Overnight	1½-2 hrs.	3 cups	10-15 min.	2 cups
Great Northern	Overnight	1½-2 hrs.	3 cups	5-10 min.	2¼ cups
Kidney	Overnight	1½-2 hrs.	3 cups	10-20 min.	2½ cups
Lentils	No soaking	30-60 min.	3 cups	No	2¼ cups
Lima	Overnight	1-1½ hrs.	2-3 cups	No	2 cups
Navy	Overnight	1½-2 hrs.	3 cups	15-20 min.	2¼ cups
Peas (dried)	Overnight	45-60 min.	3 cups	15 min.	2¼ cups
Pigeon peas	Overnight	1½-2 hrs.	3 cups	8-10 min.	3 cups
Pinto	Overnight	1½-2 hrs.	3 cups	15-20 min.	2¼ cups
Soybean	Overnight	3-4 hrs.	4 cups	15-20 min.	2 cups
Split Peas	No soaking	30-45 min.	4 cups	No	2¼ cups

Canned Beans.

Canned beans are a fast, convenient alternative to cooking from scratch. They cook up quickly with little preparation, are available in a wide variety of types, flavors and combinations and have a long shelf-life. Store a good selection of bean and lentil soups; chili's; beans in molasses, syrup and tomato sauces; mixed bean salads and other favorites. Variety is truly the spice of life, and especially a variety of foods when living under survival conditions.

Cooking Canned Beans.

- Drain off all the liquid in canned beans and rinse thoroughly to remove the salty taste. Do not use this liquid to cook with as it will create bloating and gas. Ready-to-eat beans in sauces or soups should not be drained or rinsed.
- Add canned beans to soups, stews, pasta and rice dishes for added flavor, fiber, and nutrients.

Beans — The Musical Fruit.

Beans are called the musical fruit. Soaking helps eliminate their gas-causing potential and changing the water once or twice during the early cooking process will remove more of the problem-producing sugars. Making sure they are well-cooked will also help. If you eat a diet rich in beans, you will soon develop a tolerance to them and they will no longer bother you.

RICE.

Rice is an essential staple. It can supply 55 percent of your daily food needs and more food energy than potatoes or pasta *(depending on variety.)* It is nutritious, inexpensive, easy to use and complements just about everything, and comes in a wide variety of tastes and textures.

Selecting and Storing.

Rice is classified by its size: long, medium or short-grain. Long-grain rice has a different texture when cooked than short-grain rice and is the best choice for most rice dishes. Choose packages with kernels that are clean and smooth. Don't buy packages containing kernels that are dull, dusty, broken or shrivelled. Buy your rice from a busy, reliable retailer with a high turnover. Store many different rices, including some whole grain varieties, for maximum nutrition and to prevent monotony.

White rices keep for 12 to 24 months if stored in an airtight covered container in a cool, dry, dark place. The coolness inhibits insect infestations, dryness curtails mold and darkness minimizes vitamin loss. It keeps indefinitely if frozen. Brown rice *can be stored* for only 6 months, as it is highly susceptible to rancidity when kept at room temperature. To keep longer, store at 35°- 40° F or freeze. Wild rice will keep for 12 to 24 months if stored in an airtight covered container in a cool, dry place.

Rice Math.

- 1 cup regular rice = 3 cups cooked
- 1 cup converted = 3½ cups cooked
- 1 cup instant rice = 2 cups cooked
- 1 cup brown rice = 4 cups cooked

Preparing.

- Sort through rice and discard any damaged or old kernels and remove any twigs, leaves or stones.
- Most domestic brands can and *should* be cooked *without* rinsing, especially vitamin enriched varieties, but imported brands should be rinsed before using to remove possible impurities.
- To rinse, place rice in a sieve and rinse under cold, running water until water runs clear or soak rice in a bowl with plenty of water to cover, stir the rice, then drain. Repeat until water clears.

Rice Cooking Secrets.

- Make sure the lid on the pot you are using for rice fits tightly to prevent steam from escaping.
- Frequent peeking to check on rice lets out valuable steam and may slow the cooking process. It can also cause the rice to be gritty *(hard on the inside)*. Check about 5 minutes before the end of the recommended cooking time.
- Don't stir rice *while it is cooking* as it disturbs the holes which form and allow the steam to more readily escape.

Rice Varieties	Basic Rice Cooking Methods
Brown Rice	Bring 2 cups of water to a boil. Add 1 cup of rice and stir once. Cover, reduce heat to low and simmer for 45-50 minutes. Remove from heat and let stand 5 minutes. Fluff with a fork.
Converted	Bring 2¼ cups of water to a boil. Add 1 cup of rice and stir once. Cover, reduce heat to low and simmer for 15–25 minutes. Remove from heat and let stand 5-10 minutes. Fluff with a fork.
White Rice	Bring 1½ cups of water to a boil. Add 1 cup of rice and stir once. Cover, reduce heat to low and simmer for 18 minutes. Remove from heat and let stand 5 minutes. Fluff with a fork.
Wild	Bring 2½ cups of water to a boil. Add 1 cup of rice and stir once. Cover, reduce heat to low and simmer for 40-45 minutes. Remove from heat and let stand 5 minutes. Fluff with a fork.
Asian Method	Put 1 cup of rice in a saucepan with 2 cups cold water. Bring it to a boil over high heat, cover and cook until water has been absorbed down to the level of the rice. Stir well with a spoon, *(this releases the surface starch from the kernels and produces a stickier rice),* cover and reduce heat to low; cook until grains are tender, about 15 minutes. Fluff with a fork.
Pilaf Method	In a heavy-bottomed saucepan, over medium heat, melt 2 tbsp. oil or butter. Add 1 cup of rice and stir to coat all kernels with oil. Sauté for 2 to 3 minutes, stirring constantly. Add 1½ cups boiling water for white rice, 2 cups for brown rice, 2½ cups for wild rice, then cover, and reduce heat to low and steam until tender, *(15-20 minutes for white rice, 30-45 minutes for brown and wild rice.).* Remove from heat, let stand for 5 minutes and fluff with a fork.
Baking Method	Preheat oven to 400°F. Combine 1 cup of rice and 1½ cup liquid in an ovenproof saucepan or casserole dish. On the stovetop, bring the water to a boil, stir once, cover and place in oven. Bake until rice is tender and the liquid is absorbed, about 20 minutes for long-grain white rice. Fluff with a fork. This method can be duplicated with a cast-iron Dutch oven, if oven is unavailable.

- It is best to cook rice without salt; add salt to taste after rice is done.
- For extra flavor add herbs to the water or use chicken, vegetable or beef broth or even apple juice instead of water.
- For whiter rice, try adding 1-2 tsp. of lemon juice to the cooking water.
- To prevent boil-overs add a few drops of vegetable oil to water while cooking.
- Rice is done when it is tender with no hard center.
- If your rice is too firm, yet all the liquid has been absorbed, simply add ¼ cup of hot water or broth, cover and cook on low until absorbed.

- If your rice is done but excess moisture remains, remove the cover and cook over low heat, fluffing rice with a fork until the excess liquid evaporates.
- If your rice has been scorched or burned, it is best to start over. If you can't, carefully spoon out the rice above the burned area into an ovenproof dish or pan. Cover with a single layer of soft white bread slices or onion skins. Cover these with a piece of paper towel and put a lid on the pan. Place in the oven at 250°F for 10 minutes. Then remove and discard towel, bread or onions and serve. The taste should be fine.
- To economize, mix wild rice with brown or white rice or bulgur. Cook them separately and combine just before serving as they have different cooking times.
- Fluffing just-cooked rice with a fork allows any steam left to escape and separates the grains.
- Rice cooked with acidic ingredients such as tomatoes, often requires extra liquid and longer cooking times.
- Do not let rice sit out after cooking. Store in airtight container at 30°- 40°F for one day at most.

Rice Types and Varieties.

Aromatic rice: A term used for varieties of rices with a nutty flavor and a pleasant aroma.

Basmati Rice: Available in white or brown, this aromatic long-grained rice has a wonderful nutty taste. Used in many Indian dishes.

Brown: This nutritious rice has a nutty flavor and a chewy texture. It is an excellent source of fiber and vitamin E. Because the outer shell (*the bran*) is intact, brown rice will require twice the cooking time of white rice. It is also highly susceptible to rancidity because of the oil in the bran layer. Any whole grain will go rancid unless stored under 40°F or kept frozen.

Converted/Parboiled: This rice has been steam-pressure treated to force the nutrients from the outer bran layer deep into the grain. A stable and relatively nutritious food. It has a firm texture and separates well.

Glutinous/SweetRice: Also called sticky rice, this stubby rice sticks together when cooked.

Italian Rice: A short or medium-grain rice which is high in starch and produces the creamy texture good for risotto's or rice pudding.

Instant: This rice is previously cooked and dried. To use, it must be rehydrated and reheated. Some texture and flavor are lost in the process, but it is fast *(saves fuel).*

Jasmine Rice: This long-grain rice is excellent for fried rice. It has a lovely floral aroma when cooked.

Long Grain: The most common variety — used in both North America and Western Europe. Available in white or brown, it cooks up fluffy and separates well.

Short or Medium-grain: These varieties have short, rounded kernels that cook up moist and slightly sticky. Popular for Asian dishes.

Texmati Rice: Also called American basmati rice, it is a hybrid of aromatic rice and regular long-grain varieties. Available in white or brown, it is excellent for pilafs and most dishes.

White: White rice has had the brownish outer hull removed which removes the fiber and most vitamins. Most domestic brands of rice are enriched and shouldn't be rinsed before using.

Wild: Actually not a real rice, but the seed from an aquatic grass. It is very nutritious and good tasting. Although expensive, it can be added to other rices to improve and enhance their flavor.

PASTA.

Dried pasta is another essential for your food storage pantry. It provides protein, fiber and B vitamins, as well as complex carbohydrates. It is filling, long-lasting and comes in many flavors, shapes and textures. With such a tremendous selection of pastas and sauces available to choose from, you will easily be able to enjoy a wonderful variety of tasty meals for many months from your storage cupboard.

Selecting and Storing.

- Buy plain dried pasta made with durum wheat or semolina flour.
- The new herb, spice and vegetable varieties are strongly flavored. They are excellent without a sauce but should be eaten with dishes containing meat, fish, or vegetables.
- Add some dried Asian noodles to your food storage cupboard for new tastes and textures.
- When buying dried pasta make sure packages have no holes or rips. Check boxes for evidence of insects or nibbled corners. Look for packages without a lot of broken pieces or strands. If the contents are crumbly or dusty — air has gotten in and it will be stale.
- Dried pasta will last almost indefinitely if stored in an airtight container in a cool, dry, dark place. However, dried whole wheat pasta may turn rancid if stored longer than 1 month.
- In general, plan on 3 ounces of dried pasta *per person* for a main-course serving. *(3 oz. is approximately 100 strands of dry spaghetti, or 1 cup dry penné noodles or 2 cups of dry egg noodles.)*

Dry Pasta Math.

- 3 ounces spaghetti = 1½ c. cooked
- 3 ounces elbow = 1½ c. cooked
- 1 pound dry spaghetti *(950g)* = about 7 cups cooked
- 1 pound dry elbow macaroni = about 9 cups cooked.
- Use 2 cups of sauce/lb. of pasta.

Cooking.

- Any good sized pot will make a good pasta pot or if you wish, you can invest in an actual pasta pot with a removable, perforated, inner basket that you can lift out for easy draining when the pasta is done.

- For 1 pound of pasta use about 4 quarts water. Bring water to a rapid boil, add pasta. The movement of the water will keep the noodles from sticking.
- Follow package instructions. Cooking times vary because of different combinations of flour and egg. Check a few minutes before recommended time is up for doneness. Do not overcook.
- After cooking, drain and toss immediately with sauce. Rinse pasta in cold water if it is to be used for a salad, or if it is to be handled, *(i.e. shells or lasagne)*.
- Pasta disasters are usually from overcooking or undercooking. Often, dried pasta requires less cooking time than the package recommends. Check pasta to see if it is done by biting into a piece. If it is firm but tender all the way through, it's done. Pasta that is undercooked will have a semi-solid center.
- Do not thoroughly cook any pasta that is to be cooked further in another dish. Cook the pasta for a third of the recommended cooking time as it will continue to cook and absorb more liquid in the new dish.

Pasta Cooking Secrets.

- Unsalted water will reach a boil faster than salted water. Add salt just before adding pasta. Salt toughens protein.
- Add 1 tbsp. of vegetable oil to the boiling water to keep pasta from sticking together. Also, rub a little oil around the top of the pot to prevent boil-overs.
- After adding pasta to boiling water, put a lid on the pot to speed the water's return to boiling. Remove lid when the boil has returned.
- To cook long pastas such as fettuccine or spaghetti, simply add to boiling water and, as the ends soften, press gently into the water.
- Thoroughly drain cooked pasta to prevent water clinging to pasta from diluting your sauce.
- Pasta cools quickly. To keep it warm, fill the serving bowl with hot water to warm the bowl, pour out and dry, then add hot pasta.
- If you don't have the same pasta called for in a recipe, use one with a similar shape.

Pasta Types and Varieties.

The best pastas to have on hand are capellini, egg noodles, elbow macaroni, farfalle, fettuccine, fusilli, penné, rigatoni, shells, spaghetti and vegetable noodles. For variety, buy many different flavors and types. Choose from regular durum pastas, vegetable flavored pastas, egg pastas, herb flavored pastas, and whole grain pastas, etc.

In general the shape of the pasta determines the cooking method and the type of sauce to use. Buy lots of different pastas for variety:
for soups use: capelli d'angelo (angel-hair), or ruote *(wagonwheels)*.
for stuffing or for baking use: canneloni, lumache *(shells)*, ziti tagliati or manicotti.
for layering use: lasagne.

with light sauces or tomato sauce use: spaghetti, fettuccine, linguine, tagliatelle, or vermicelli.
with chunky tomato, vegetable or meat sauces use: hollow pastas, ones with ridges or spirals that sauce will cling to, such as farfalle, fusilli, macaroni, penné, rigatoni, shells, spaghetti, or ziti tagliati.
for quick heat and serve meals use: canned ravioli, tortellini, fusilli, etc.

GRAINS.

Whole grains are one of the most valuable foods you can eat from a nutritional standpoint. They are rich in proteins, fiber, carbohydrates, good fats, vitamins and minerals. They are also delicious and easy to prepare. Their only real drawback is our unfamiliarity with what to do with them and how to prepare them.

You will not be sorry to have added a variety of grains to your food storage pantry, as they will go a long way in providing you and your family with an excellent food source should there be prolonged food shortages.

Selecting and Storing.

You can buy grains pre-packaged or from a bulk retail store. To prevent *large* losses due to spoilage, buy small amounts of each variety. Buy from a retailer that has a high turnover of grain products and clean, cool storage facilities.

Whole kernels of grain complete with the oil-rich germ tend to turn rancid fairly quickly when stored at room temperatures and exposed to the air. Keep your whole grains in airtight, glass jars or metal containers. Store in a cool, dry place, or refrigerate in a moistureproof container *(or at 30°- 40°F)* or freeze. Processed kernels (*with bran and germ removed*) will last for a year if stored in an airtight container in a cool, dry place.

Preparing.

Spread grain out on a paper towel and remove any chaff, twigs, pebbles or other debris you might find. After cleaning, rinse. Whole grains should always be sorted and rinsed but processed grains can be used directly from the package.

Cooking Grains.

(see chart on the following page). Cooking times vary depending on type of cookware used, cooking temperature and age of the grain. Check for doneness at least 5-10 minutes before the recommended cooking time. Don't be surprised if grain is done early, or takes longer than the times listed on the package.

If you're new to cooking grains, follow the package instructions for making breakfast cereals, pilafs and for steeping and simmering grain. Also, invest in a simple, grain cookbook. Try a new recipe each week. Become proficient in your cooking *before* year 2000.

Types of Grain Amount: 1 cup	Add Water	Cook Covered	Let Stand	Yield	Main Use
Amaranth	1½ cups	20 min.	don't	2 cups	Cereal
Barley: pearl	2½ cups	40 min.	5 min.	3½ cups	Side dish, pilafs
Barley: pot	2½ cups	1¼ hours	10 min.	3¼ cups	Soups
Bulgur: pilaf	2 cups	20 min	5 min.	3 cups	Side dish, salad
Bulgur: porridge	4 cups	20 min*		3 cups	Cereal
Corn: hominy	5 cups	20 min.		4¼ cups	Side dish
Corn: polenta	4 cups	25 min.		4 cups	Side dish
Couscous	1¾ cups	1 min.	5 min.	2¼ cups	Side dish
Kasha	2 cups	15 min.	5 min.	3½ cups	Pilaf
Millet	2 cups	25 min.	5 min.	4 cups	Side dish, soups
Oats: rolled	2 cups	5-8 min.	2 min.	1¾ cups	Cereal, baking
Quinoa	2 cups	15 min.	5 min.	3½ cups	Side dish
Rye: Flakes	2 cups	25 min.		2½ cups	Cereal, baking
Triticale	2 cups	35 min		2¼ cups	Cereal, casserole
Wheat: Berries	2 cups	50 min.	10 min.	2¾ cups	Casserole
Wheat: Cracked	2 cups	25 min.	5 min.	3 cups	Cereal, side dish

Basic Cooking Method.

- Bring water to a boil in a 2-quart, non-stick saucepan.
- Stir in 1 cup of uncooked grain.
- Reduce heat to low, cover and simmer for recommended time.
- Test for doneness.
- Let stand for the specified time.
- Salt *after* cooking, *but only if necessary.*

Grain Cooking Secrets.

- Always measure the grain and liquid accurately and follow package or recipe directions.
- Add seeds, nuts, canned fish, meat or beans for a complete meal.
- Some grains can be soaked overnight in a cool place *(30°-40°F)* to shorten cooking time.
- To prevent grains from sticking to the pot and scorching use a pot with a non-stick surface and a heavy bottom.

FLOURS.

Of all the ***Back to Basics*** foods and cookery suggestions, a variety of flours and the ability to make your own bread, are among the most critical to your nutritional health.

With potential runs on grocery stores almost a certainty and Y2k related food disruptions resulting in empty grocery shelves possibly lasting several months, bread or flour may be in short supply.

For anyone serious about being prepared, the ability to make bread without an oven will be essential. With a one or two burner camp-stove, a cast-iron dutch oven or skillet with a lid, you can easily prepare simple, healthy, tasty breads, biscuits, scones, flatbreads and even desserts. Camping stores carry camp ovens or sheet-metal ovens that are designed to work on a regular campstove. With these you can prepare anything you would make in your own oven.

The following is an illustration of one of the "*Outback ovens*". They come with a folding reflective hood to concentrate the heat, a diffuser plate to diffuse the heat and a metal riser to lift the oven off of the direct heat. The oven has a thermometer on the top which is viewable through a hole in the hood. They come in four sizes and are priced under $100.

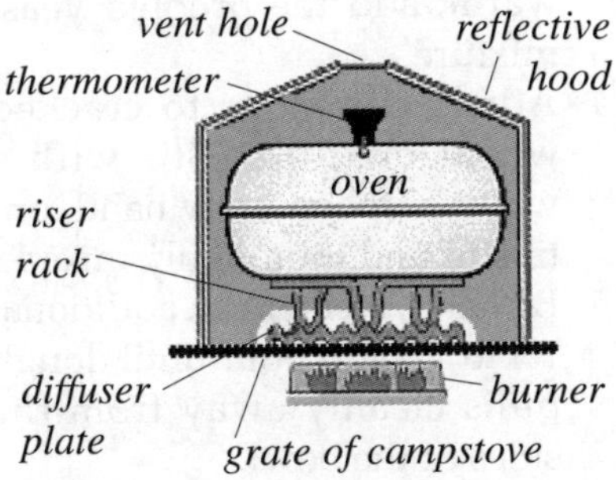

Selecting and Storing.

It is very important to select the right flour, as it affects the taste, texture and nutritional content of bread. Whole grain flours are superior in nutrition, retaining more B-vitamins and fiber than white flours, which are refined and enriched. However, a bread made only with whole wheat flour can be dense and difficult to digest. Try using a combination of all-purpose and whole wheat flours for maximum nutrition, as well as for good taste and texture.

White flours can be stored at room temperature in *airtight* metal, glass or food grade plastic containers for up to 1 year. You can extend the shelf-life to 2 or more years by storing in a cool, dry place, or chill at 30°- 40°F, or freezing.

Whole grain — flours that contain the grain's germ — will turn rancid in about a month at room temperatures. Buy them in small packages, keep them separate from your white flours and store in moistureproof, airtight containers at cold temperatures. To prevent rapid spoilage, do not store whole wheat flour in plastic containers unless they are NSF-approved, acrylic food grade containers.

Don't forget to stock these critical ingredients: baking powder, baking soda, canned milk, cream of tartar, dried eggs, salt, shortening, sugar or honey, sourdough starter and yeast. Also, to your food pantry add flavor enhancers such as herbs or spices; dried fruits such as raisins, cranberries, or currents; seeds such as poppy, sesame, caraway or sunflower; and sprouting grains like wheat or rye, etc.

Basic Breads.

There are two main types of bread: **yeasted** *(made with yeast)* and **unyeasted** *(made with baking powder or another leavening agent instead of yeast).* White or whole wheat loaves, buns, rolls, croissants are yeasted breads. Corn breads, flatbreads, biscuits and scones are unyeasted.

All breads are made with 3 to 5 basic ingredients: flour, leavening agent, liquid, salt or sweetener and fat. The addition of herbs, seeds, sprouts, grains, mashed potatoes, sundried tomatoes, grated carrots, onions or zucchini can transform these simple ingredients into a world of flavors. Breadmaking may soon become one of the most important, self-reliance skills you can develop!

Basic *Yeasted* Breadmaking.

Here's a great recipe for a cracked wheat bread that we were able to refine with practice — a recipe that works well **in a Dutch oven on a campstove**. We used me *(Ken)* as the guinea pig, as I had never made bread in my life. We thought that if I could do it, anyone could! This recipe makes enough delicious bread for 4 hearty appetites.

¾ cup cracked wheat
½ cup raisins
¼ cup firmly packed brown sugar
1 teaspoon salt
1½ tablespoon butter, margarine or ghee
1 cup boiling water
1 pkg. active dry yeast
⅛ cup warm water for yeast
2½ to 3 cups all purpose flour
1 tablespoon vegetable oil

1 Start with all your ingredients at room temperature or warmer *(70°- 75°F)*. Cool temperatures will cause slow rising time.
2 Check or prove yeast before adding other ingredients by mixing 1 package with ⅓ cup *warm* water *(110°F)*, 1 tsp. sugar and 1 tsp. flour. Stir and set aside. It should bubble and froth within 10 minutes. If it doesn't froth the yeast is dead. Buy your yeast with the longest expiration dates you can. The active, dry yeast is best and lasts for a full 15 months refrigerated in an airtight, moistureproof container. Yeast can be stored longer, but weakens with age.
3 In a large bowl, mix cracked wheat, raisins, brown sugar, salt, butter and 1 cup boiling water. Mix well and allow to cool until just warm *(110°F)*. Once the mixture cools to just warm, add the proofed yeast mixture.
4 Add 1 cup flour to cracked wheat mixture. Stir with a wooden spoon or by hand, until stiff and thoroughly mixed.
5 By hand, blend in an additional 1¼ to 1½ cup flour until dough pulls cleanly away from the sides of the bowl.
6 On floured surface, knead in another ¼-½ cup of flour. Knead until dough is smooth and elastic, about 10 minutes. Don't feel that you have to add flour until the dough isn't at all sticky or tacky inside; the finished bread will just be a little lighter. *(Dust your hands and the surface you are kneading on with flour to keep dough from sticking to them)*.
7 Kneading is very important to the success of your bread. Under-kneaded bread doesn't rise properly and is coarse and streaky.

8 To knead, place your hands side by side and press down on the dough with the heel of your hand. Flatten the dough to a thickness of ½″.
9 With both hands, take the edge furthest from you and fold it back on itself, toward you.
10 Turn the dough a quarter turn, then with the heel of your hands flatten it out to a ½″ thickness.
11 Repeat this for 7 to 10 minutes until the dough is soft and smooth. Several times in this process, lift the dough off the board and slam it back down. It's good for it! If necessary, add a little flour to prevent sticking but too much will cause bread to be heavy. Finally, poke the dough with your finger; when it almost fills back in, the dough is ready for rising. *(It is easy to under-knead but almost impossible to over-knead dough by hand. The more you knead the dough, the nicer the finished bread will be.)* If you don't work up a bit of a sweat, you aren't kneading hard enough!
12 Place dough lump in a lightly greased, large bowl and cover loosely with plastic wrap and a cloth towel. Place dough in a warm *(80°- 85°F)*, draft-free place for 1 hour to double in size. *(Bread made with baking powder or soda requires no kneading or rising time.)*
13 When the dough has doubled in size, remove it from the bowl and punch it with your fist to remove excess gas bubbles. Knead it again until smooth. Divide it into two equal lumps of dough.
14 Shape each lump and place in a lightly greased 7″ foil pie plate. Cover dough and baking pan with a cloth and let it rise a second time. It should double in size within 45-60 min.
15 Prepare your Dutch oven by wrapping heavy-duty aluminum foil over the lid to reflect the heat back to the bread. If possible, get barbecue-strength foil.
16 We bought a 4 quart Dutch oven because it seemed the best size for most meals. However, most recommend the larger 6 or 8 quart size. The 4 quart Dutch oven is 8¾″ in diameter at the bottom; so a 7″ foil pie plate fits perfectly, with plenty of room for air circulation.
17 We used another 7″ foil pie plate with small triangles cut out of the side, as shown below.

The holes prevent the hot air from being trapped under the upside-down plate, creating hot spots.
18 Take a piece of aluminum foil 18″ x 18″ and fold in half and again in half until you have a multi-layered hot pad about 4½″x 4½″. Place the foil hot pad between lower plate and upper plate containing the bread loaf. This prevents the bottom of the loaf from burning, while the top browns.

19 The following diagram shows how we set it all up:

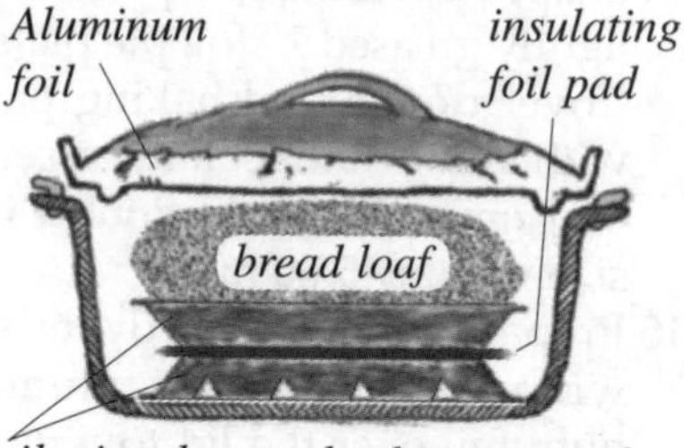

foil pie plates, the lower one has triangular holes cut in the side for air movement. Caution: foil edges are very sharp, so don't cut yourself.

20 Preheat Dutch oven to 350°F. Place an oven thermometer inside as shown to set the burn rate of your campstove. Arrange everything just as it will be when you bake your bread, to get the most accurate reading.

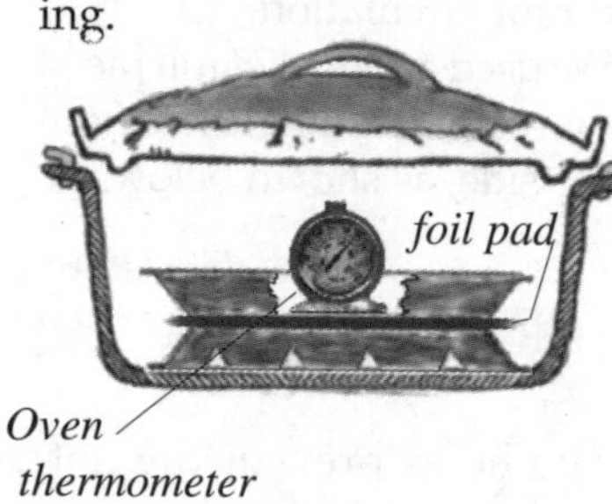

21 Once bread has again doubled in size, brush each loaf with a little vegetable oil or butter or olive oil, or . . .

22 In our Dutch oven, there is very little clearance between the sides and the foil pie plate with the raw dough, so I use a kitchen tong to hold one side of the foil pan and gently drop it in the oven. Put the lid on and make note of the time.

23 Bake for 35 minutes. It doesn't hurt to stand guard over the process as the bread bakes. If you smell even a hint of burning, lift the lid and take a quick peek — you can easily avoid a ruined loaf.

24 Once the bread has cooked for 35 minutes, flip the bread loaf over in the pie plate and bake for another ten minutes to brown the top. Complicated procedure, but it works! Enjoy.

Basic *Unyeasted* Breadmaking.

We wanted a bread that could be fried in a skillet on a campstove without any fancy techniques or equipment. To that end, we tried a lot of Bannock and skillet recipes with little success. The problem is that most backpacking recipes ask for hot coals to be placed on the lid of a Dutch oven, or the skillet to be set near hot coals while the bread bakes. Not too practical for in-home, campstove cooking!

While experimenting, we had a lot of failures and felt that some of our loaves could give bullet-proof vest manufacturers some pretty serious competition, but we found a recipe for a Bannock bread that works perfectly every time. The secret is in the ***liquidity*** of the dough.

2 cups all purpose flour
4 teaspoons baking powder
½ teaspoon salt
2 teaspoons brown sugar
1½ cups water
2 tablespoons shortening
½ cup of raisins (optional)

- Combine all dry ingredients in a bowl.
- Just before adding water to the dry ingredients, put a 10" skillet on a medium heat to preheat.
- Gradually add enough water to make a thick batter that will ***pour out*** level. Mix rapidly with a spoon until smooth.
- Melt half of the shortening in the skillet *(1 tablespoon)*. Be sure to cover the sides of the skillet as well as the bottom with oil.
- Pour the dough into the skillet. If the consistency is correct, it will flow into a level cake about 1¼" deep.
- When cooking, move the pan around on the burner so that the loaf will brown evenly rather than burn in one spot. Use an egg turner to flip the loaf over when the bottom of the loaf is golden brown.
- Cook until a toothpick poked into the middle comes out clean.
- To avoid excess moisture, cool on a cake rack when done.

This is a very versatile recipe. For a different taste, substitute one cup of whole wheat flour or multi-grain flour for one cup of the all-purpose flour. Add ¼ cup of cracked wheat, if you like, or some fruit *(cooking time increases slightly with addition of fruit)*.

Using Cast-iron for baking.

- Use only genuine cast-iron, as steel, pig-iron or aluminum can warp, or develop hot spots which cause food to burn and stick. A 6-quart cast-iron Dutch oven will serve delectable, one-pot meals for 4-6 people. The 8-quart size will hold a cake pan, loaf pan or round bread loaf for baking. Any hardware or chain department store can order one for you if you can't readily find one.
- Season and clean your Dutch oven according to the manufacturers directions. Done right, they develop a nonstick surface.
- Bring them up to temperature slowly. Putting them on too high a heat when cold can cause them to break. Also, don't drop your cast-iron cookware. They can be exceptionally hard on your feet or can shatter.
- Check the temperature of your Dutch oven with an oven thermometer. Experiment to get the temperature and cooking times accurate and to become familiar with your campstove. How does it *sound* when the baking temperature is just right?
- Don't leave your Dutch oven lid covered with foil. It traps moisture and causes the lid to rust. Re-season the lid, if necessary.

Best Flour Varieties to Store.

All-purpose flour: A blend of high-gluten hard wheat and low-gluten soft wheat. It is milled from the inner part of the wheat kernel and doesn't contain the germ or the bran. Most all-purpose flours are *enriched* with niacin, riboflavin and thiamin. Use all-purpose flour for most baked goods and combine with whole wheat for yeast and quick breads.

It is available in two varieties: bleached and unbleached, which can be used interchangeably but unbleached is best for bread.

Whole wheat flour: Made by grinding the whole grain, including the germ and bran. Because it contains more fiber, B-vitamins and natural oils, it can turn rancid quite easily. Check the date on the package for freshness and store properly. Also, check *Nutritional Information* for protein levels of flour. Use flours with 12-14 grams of protein per cup for yeast breads; and 9-11 grams for quick breads.

Multigrain flour: A blend of flours such as cracked wheat, cracked rye and whole flax seed. Gives breads a rich, wholesome flavor. Treat the same as whole wheat flour.

Self-rising flour: Use self-rising flour only for quick breads not for yeast breads; and make sure you don't buy flour specifically made for breadmaking machines — it will work and is higher in gluten, but requires more kneading.

Cornmeal: Ground from whole corn kernels. It contains both the bran and heart. It is coarser and less refined than corn flour. To make cornbread or muffins, it is necessary to add wheat flour *(for the gluten)* so it will rise.

For some new flavors: Add small amounts of these specialty flours. Amaranth *(¼ c.)* for a slightly sweet taste; Barley *(¼ c.)* for a sweet, malt-like taste; Brown rice *(¼ c.)* for a sweet taste; Buckwheat *(¼ c.)* for a nutty taste; Rye *(½-¾ c.)* for a tangy, slightly sour taste; or Triticale *(½ c.)* for a tangy taste.

Bread Problems.

Dough fails to rise: Yeast may be inactive. Check expiration date on yeast. Proofing water was too hot and killed the yeast. Used too little flour or oil, or too few eggs.

Bread tastes yeasty: Too much yeast was used in the recipe — check amount used. Allow bread to rise to only double its size, no more — to slow the rising process, find a cooler place for dough to rise.

Bread is heavy and dense: Too much flour in recipe. Reduce amount of flour used. Knead less flour into dough through the kneading process.

Crumb is uneven: Not enough salt or the bread was baked at too low a temperature. Add a little more salt to your recipe. Check your oven with an accurate oven thermometer.

Bread is crumbly: Insufficient gluten developed. Knead dough more. Allow dough to rise longer. Use a higher-gluten flour.

Bread is colorless: Definitely undercooked. Remove the semi-finished loaf from its pan and return to the oven for a few minutes, until it browns. Bake directly on the oven rack.

Bottom is burned: Baked with heat too high. Place baking dish in middle of oven or where heat is even. Make sure there is a space for air circulation beneath the bread pan. When using glass bakeware, decrease the oven temperature or baking time.

Bread is tasteless and coarse: Salt was omitted. Add salt.

Campstove Cookin'

Assuring That You'll Have Food.
In a survival situation, the ability to prepare easy but nutritious meals becomes critical. Many people *will not* have had time to place orders *or wait* for deliveries of MRE's, dehydrated foodstuffs, or pre-packaged survival kits. Our objective in this section, therefore, is to provide you with suggestions for meals that you can prepare from foods which are *presently* available on the shelves of your local supermarket.

Looking at shelves full of dried and canned beans, rices, grains, pastas and sauces, soups, flours, tinned meats and canned vegetables is **your** ***"guarantee"*** that you and your loved ones will be able to eat and survive any crisis. Also, we sincerely encourage everyone — *after* you have provided for your family — to put aside food that can be shared with others who are less prepared than you, and find themselves in great need.

Campstove Cookin'.
You will notice that most of the menu suggestions and recipes are designed to be cooked on a campstove. Some will be ready to eat in less than five minutes, but on the average, most meals cook up in about fifteen. However, preparing meals such as bean soup or bread will require significantly longer cooking times but are well worth the additional fuel consumption.

We *strongly urge* everyone to try to get some type of campstove *(i.e. 1 or 2 burner)* or some other fuel source *(i.e. sterno)* over which you can, ***at least,*** boil water for instant oatmeal or instant cup-a-soup or heat up a can of pasta, beans, stew or ready-to-eat, canned soups. Many canned food items require only a few minutes of heating to be ready to eat and the fuel consumption is minimal. *Note: the ability to eat hot food will help you keep up your strength and better cope with any crisis.*

The following section provides breakfast, lunch, dinner and snack suggestions, sample menu ideas, and a few simple recipes. Because we cannot know *if or when* fresh produce or dairy products will be available in your area, all suggestions and recipes rely completely on canned, bottled or packaged food that you can easily store.

The most important factor when buying and preparing meals is to have lots of variety. This will prevent yourself and family members from becoming bored, depressed and unable to cope with demands.

Breakfast.
It is essential that you start every day with breakfast, because you must keep your energy levels up and provide your body with adequate fuel to meet the demands of everyday survival. Try to start

each day with a warm breakfast, but if you can't, at least have a breakfast bar with dried fruit.

Breakfast Suggestions:
Pancakes, cold cereal *(eat dry or with milk made from powder)*, instant oatmeal or other cereals made with hot water, cooked cereals such as Red River cereal or cream of wheat, peanut butter on a cracker, hot scones or biscuits, fruit bars or granola bars eaten alone or with dried fruit or applesauce, meal-replacement bars or drinks, etc..

Sample Breakfast Menus:
1 Fruit or granola bar with a bowl of applesauce, canned fruit or fruit cocktail.
2 Instant flavored oatmeal *(with or without milk)* and dried fruits, such as diced apricots or dates.
3 Pancakes *(any variety)* add diced fruit, sunflower seeds, etc. Serve with syrup or applesauce.

Lunch.

Most lunches can be quick and light or if you prefer you can have the largest meal of the day at noon and profit from the energy boost. Quick and light meals are suggested here. Heartier meals can be found under Supper choices. They can be used interchangeably.

Lunch Suggestions:
Instant cup-a-soup, flaked ham, chicken, or turkey luncheon meats or tuna on crackers, biscuits or bread, ready-to-eat canned pastas or soups, boxed macaroni and cheese, chili, beans in sauce, etc.

Sample Lunch Menus:
1 Macaroni and cheese, melba toast with luncheon ham flakes.
2 Can of well-drained tuna mixed with cream of mushroom soup poured hot over rice or biscuits.
3 Instant cup-a-soup with cheese or wheat crackers.
4 Canned pasta *(ravioli, spagetti, rigationi)* with herbed crackers.

Supper.

Make the supper meal substantial enough to provide enough energy to help keep you warm throughout the night, if it is cold. Also, a tasty, hot meal helps keep everyone from slipping into despair or apathy. Always have some bread, biscuits or crackers at this meal, and finish the meal with a dessert like canned pears, peaches, or jar of cherries or vanilla, chocolate or rice pudding with a cookie.

Supper Suggestions:
Canned stew and hot biscuits, ready-to-eat chunky soups, any pasta and sauce combination, beans served over rice or noodles, canned meat with rice and canned vegetables, lentils, grains, etc..

Sample Supper Menu:
1 Spaghetti with chunky vegetable sauce or meat sauce and bread or cheese crackers.
2 Clam chowder soup with mixed vegetables and added clams.
3 Macaroni and cheese with chunks of canned ham or tuna and stewed tomatoes.
4 Can of chili over white or brown rice with can of mexicorn.

Snacks and Beverages.

Plan on having a small snack about mid-morning, mid-afternoon and your favorite comfort food in the evening. During a crisis situation, small snacks provide a constant energy level between meals, plus it is something to look forward to. Make sure that you and everyone else in your family drinks at least 3 glasses of ***water*** each day. This is critical to ward off dehydration or you could face a serious health crisis. Also, try to limit coffee and tea as they are diuretics and can cause you to dehydrate quickly. Use vegetable and fruit juices for quick energy boosts.

Cloud Nine Bean Soup Mix

Combine 1 lb *(500g)* each of:

dried Great Northern beans
dried pinto beans
dried navy beans
dried red kidney beans
dried black turtle beans
dried black-eyed peas
dried green split pea
dried yellow split pea
dried red lentils
pearl barley

In a large bowl, mix the beans and lentils thoroughly, then scoop out 2 cup *(500mL)* portions and put in small zip-lock bags or jars. These will be your basic soup mix starter. Makes a great gift to share with friends in need.

To make soup, you will need

1 package of soup mix (2 cups beans)
8 cups of water
1 large onion/ ¼ cup dried onion
1 clove garlic/1 tbsp minced garlic
½ tsp salt (opt)
Optional items to add:
1 canned ham, cubed for soup
1 can (19oz) tomatoes (whole or diced, stewed or any flavor)
1 can (4oz) chopped green chilies
You may also add white or wild rice and whole green and yellow peas.

Prepare dried beans using the quick or slow soak methods.

To start soup, cover the soaked and drained beans with water, bring to boil for 10 minutes *(lid on)*, then reduce heat and simmer for 45 minutes until the larger, firmer beans are beginning to get tender. Add onion, garlic, salt and ham cubes if desired. Simmer for another 45 minutes. You may now add tomatoes *(including juice)* and chopped green chilies, then simmer for another 15 minutes. Stir occasionally to blend flavors. Makes 8 cups of soup. *(Don't use a cast-iron pot if you are adding tomatoes; they react with the cast-iron and will cause a funny taste).*

Spanish Rice

1 cup long-grain white rice, uncooked
1 can (10oz) condensed onion soup
1 can (10oz) sliced mushrooms, drained
1¼ cups water
1 cup Mexican-style stewed tomatoes (with juice) or canned plum tomatoes, cut up with juice

In a large saucepan or skillet, combine the first four ingredients. Simmer, covered over low to medium heat for about 25-30 minutes or until rice is tender and liquid is absorbed. Add tomatoes and heat thoroughly. Makes 4 servings. Chunks of ham, salmon, or tuna can be added if desired. For a hotter version, season with red pepper flakes or add 1 cup fresh chopped sweet red and green peppers, celery and onion, if available, or use ¼ cup dehydrated flakes of each. For a different flavor, replace water with chicken or beef broth.

Red Pepper Polenta
1 cup cornmeal
1 cup cold water
¼ tsp. salt
¼ tsp. red pepper flakes
1½ cups vegetable broth
2 tbsp. parmesan cheese
1 can of white chicken (283g) (opt.)
1 can mexicorn niblets (optional)

Whisk the first 4 ingredients together in a medium bowl. Bring the broth to a boil in a medium-sized pot. Then slowly add the cornmeal mixture while constantly stirring with the whisk. Reduce the heat to low and stir the mixture with a wooden spoon until it begins to thicken. Simmer mixture on medium heat for 10-15 minutes, stirring frequently until mix is the consistency of cooked cereal. Stir in cheese, cover, remove from heat and let stand for 5 minutes. Serve alone, with beans or rice or heat canned chicken and niblets corn. Makes 4 servings.

Chili n' Pasta
3 cups (8 oz.) rotini, uncooked
1 large onion/ ¼ cup dried onion
1 can (15oz) spicy chili beans, undrained
1 can (14oz) diced or stewed tomatoes, undrained
1 tsp. chili powder
½ tsp cumin
1 can white chicken meat (optional)

In a skillet, stir in the chili beans, tomatoes, onion, chili powder and cumin. Simmer until flavors are well-blended. *(Add chicken meat now, if desired).* Heat thoroughly. Prepare rotini according to package directions, drain pasta and serve chili sauce over noodles. Makes 4 servings.

Creamy Chicken and Mushrooms
1 can condensed Cream of Mushroom soup
½ cup milk
1½ cups (1 can) sliced mushrooms (drained)
1 small onion/¼ cup dried onion
1 clove garlic minced/1 tbsp of minced dried garlic
1 can of white chicken meat (283g)
6 oz. of linguine, fettucine, spaghetti white rice or wild rice combo.

In a large skillet combine soup, milk, sliced mushrooms, onion, and garlic. Heat on medium, until flavors are blended, then add chicken. Heat thoroughly. Serve over pasta or rice. Makes 4 servings. *(This recipe can be perked up with 2 tbsp. of dry sherry or ¼ tsp. of red pepper flakes).*

Substitutions and Equivalents

What can I use instead?

At some point, you will probably find yourself short of a particular, but much needed ingredient and will have to improvise from what you have on hand. The most important substitutions you're likely to need have been included.

Abbreviations.

tsp = teaspoon • Tbl = tablespoon • c = cup • pt = pint • qt = quart • gal = gallon • ml = milliliters • l = liter • gm = grams • kg = kilogram °F = Fahrenheit • °C = Celsius

Most Helpful Substitutions.

1 small onion = 1 Tbl dehydrated flakes or instant minced onion
1 large onion = ¼ cup dehydrated flakes or instant minced onion
1 clove of garlic = 1/8 tsp garlic powder *or* ½ tsp instant minced garlic *or* ¼ teaspoon garlic juice.
1 egg = 2½ Tbl dried egg powder + 2½ Tbl of water.
1 cup milk = ½ can evaporated milk + ½ cup water.
prepared mustard = 1 tsp dried mustard + ½ tsp water + 2 drops vinegar = ½ tsp mustard.
ketchup = ½ cup tomato sauce + 2 Tbl sugar + 1 Tbl vinegar + 1/8 tsp *each* ground allspice and cloves.
1 cup tomato juice = ½ cup tomato sauce + ½ cup water.
2 cup tomato sauce = ¾ cup tomato paste + 1 cup water.
4 Tbl of fresh vegetables = 2 Tbl dried pieces *or* 1½ Tbl vegetable flakes *or* 1 Tbl vegetable powder.

Baking Ingredient Substitutions.

1 tsp baking powder = ½ tsp cream of tarter + ¼ tsp baking soda *or* 4 tsp quick-cooking tapioca
1 Tbl arrowroot = 1½ Tbl all-purpose flour *or* 2¼ tsp cornstarch
1 Tbl flour *(for thickening)* = ½ Tbl cornstarch, potato starch, rice starch, or arrowroot.
1 cake compressed yeast = 1 packet or 2 tsp of active dry yeast.
1 cup brown sugar = 1 cup granulated sugar + 2 Tbl molasses
1 cup butter = 7/8 cup corn or vegetable oil + ½ tsp salt *or* 14 Tbl lard or solid shortening + ½ tsp salt.
1 Tbl fresh herbs = 1 tsp dried herbs
1 tsp lemon juice = ¼ tsp vinegar

Eggs—*for 1 egg substitute:*

1 Tbl arrowroot powder + 3 Tbl liquid *or* 1 Tbl white vinegar plus ½ c. of milk *or* 2 tbsp liquid + 2 Tbl flour + ½ Tbl fat + 2 Tbl baking powder *or* 1 Tbl garbanzo flour + 1 Tbl oil *or* 1 Tbl lecithin granules + 3 Tbl liquid *or* 2 egg whites *(for baking or thickening)* or ¼ cup of liquid eggs for each large egg.

Dairy—*for 1 cup of milk substitute:*

1 cup milk = ½ cup evaporated milk plus ½ cup water *or* 1/3 cup dry nonfat (skim) milk + ¾ cup water *or* 1 cup buttermilk = 1 cup milk + 1 ¾ Tbl cream of tarter *or* 1 cup sour milk = 1 cup milk with 1 Tbl lemon juice or white vinegar. Let stand for 5 minutes.

Seed or nut milk = grind ½ - ¾ cup of sunflower or sesame seeds, almonds or cashews, then blend with water into milk and soak.

Do not use sweetened condensed milk in place of evaporated or dry milk.

Sweetener—*1 cup substitution:*

1 cup of sugar = 1 cup firmly packed brown sugar ***or*** 1¾ cups confectioners' sugar, ***or*** ½ cup honey or maple syrup ***or*** use 2/3 cup date butter *(soak dates or date pieces in a little hot water until soft, then blend until they are smooth.)*

Table of Equivalent Measurements.

1 teaspoon = 80 *drops* • 1/3 *tablespoon*

1 tablespoon = 3 *teaspoons* • ½ *fluid ounce*

¼ cup = 12 *teaspoons* • 4 *tablespoons* • 2 *fluid ounces*

½ cup = 24 *teaspoons* • 8 *tablespoons* • 4 *fluid ounces* • ¼ *pint*

1 cup = 48 *teaspoons* • 16 *tablespoons* • 8 *fluid ounces* • ½ *pint* • ¼ *quart* • 237 *milliliters (250 ml = ¼ liter)*

1 fluid ounce = 6 *teaspoons* • 2 *tablespoons* • 30 *milliliters*

1 fluid pint = 2 *cups* • 16 *fluid ounces* • ½ *fluid quart* • 474 *milliliters (500 ml = ½ liter)*

1 fluid quart = 4 *cups* • 32 *fluid ounces* • 2 *fluid pints* • ¼ fluid gallon • 946 *milliliters (0.946 liters)*

1 fluid gallon = 16 *cups* • 8 pints • 128 *fluid ounces* • 4 *fluid quarts* • 3,780 *milliliters (3.78 liters)*

1 liter = 1,000 *milliliters* • 1.06 *liquid quarts* • 4.22 *cups* • 33.3 *liquid ounces.*

Dry Measurements.

1 pinch = 1/8 teaspoon *approx.*

1½ teaspoons = ½ tablespoon

3 teaspoons = 1 tablespoon

2 tablespoons = 1 ounce

¼ cup = 4 tablespoons

1/3 cup = 5 tablespoons + 1 teaspoon

½ cup = 8 tablespoons

2/3 cup = 10 tablespoons + 2 teaspoon

¾ cup = 12 tablespoons

1 cup = 16 tablespoons

2 cups = 1 pint

4 cups = 1 quart

8 quarts = 1 peck*

4 pecks = 1 bushel*

1 ounce = 28 grams

16 ounces *(oz)* = 1 pound *(lb)* = 454 grams

1 kilogram = 2.2 lbs

(apply this measurement to larger fruits and vegetables, not berries.)*

American/English Conversions.

1 U.S. tsp *(5 ml)* = 1 English tsp *(5 ml)*

1 U.S. Tbl *(14.2 ml)* = 4/5 English Tbl

1¼ U.S. Tbl = 1 English Tbl *(17.7 ml)*

1 U.S. cup *(8 oz)* = 4/5 English cup

1¼ U.S. cups = 1 English cup *(10 Imperial oz)*

1 U.S. pint = 5/8 Imperial pint

2½ U.S. cups *(5 ml)* = 1 Imperial pint *(20 oz)*

Note: When substituting a liquid for a solid or dry ingredient, reduce other liquids and bake slightly longer than recipe times at a lower temperature (*by about 25 degrees*).

Last Minute – Low Budget Preparations

Everyone Can Be Prepared.
While we were writing this book we spoke to many different people about the need to prepare. Some were unaware of the potential problems that could occur with Y2k and were grateful for the information and the time to prepare. Others believed the government or some computer genius would fix it long before it affected them, and saw no need, *at this time*, to be overly concerned. Many others we spoke to saw the wisdom in preparing but because they were on fixed or low incomes expressed great apprehension about how they could afford to prepare.

Whether you are a senior, young single adult, couple, single mom or family of four or more, everyone can be prepared for potential Y2k disruptions and do it without spending a fortune.

How Long to Prepare For.
No matter what your budget or circumstances, to ensure your safety and survival, you must have water and food. To make life more bearable, you will also need light and the ability to boil water and heat your food. Plan to be totally self-reliant for an *absolute minimum* of one month. It would, however, be far better to prepare for three months and better yet for six months. *If*, Y2k causes a meltdown or even a partial meltdown of our essential services, people will need to fend for themselves for at least one to three months before the military can be mobilized throughout the entire country to meet the needs of everyone.

During the first few months of the new year, it is conceivable that the military, national guard, police and reservists will be on full-time duty to combat looting or rioting, as well as to suppress civil disobedience brought about by hungry, thirsty and frightened citizens. Even now, throughout both Canada and the U.S., military maneuvers under the guise of *"anti-terrorist training"* are, in reality, focused on civil unrest and mob control. The providing of water, food and sanitation, will not be their first priority!

Me or My Community?
It isn't selfish to prepare for yourself and your family ***first***. In fact, it would be a serious mistake ***not*** to make sure that you and yours are taken care of first — *after all, your family is your responsibility!*

If you don't prepare, you are at the mercy of whoever is in control and subject to what they do or don't do; or can or can't do. Your life may be at stake, and you can't afford to assume that someone else will be there right away to help you, your family or even your community. The real question is . . . *How can you help others, if you, yourself, are helpless and in desperate need?*

We urge everyone to get involved in any neighborhood or church efforts to help meet the needs of others who may be unable to prepare because of age, illness, or finances — ***after*** you have completed your own preparations. The most vulnerable will be the seniors, the disabled or ill, single mothers with young children, the poor and the unemployed.

Guideline for Preparing.

Some survival lists suggest storing large amounts of 4 ingredients *(flour, dry milk, salt and honey)* but unless you're able to bake bread this would be pretty unappetizing if uncooked and you'd experience appetite fatigue after just one meal. Build your food cupboard around canned foods *(soups, beans, pastas, meats, etc.)* and foods that require little or no fuel to prepare *(like cup-of-soups, instant oatmeal, granola or fruit bars)*. Stock items that are simple to prepare and stock lots of different flavors for variety.

The One Person – One Month Plan.

A single friend purchased a single mantle propane lantern, a single burner propane campstove and 20 small *(16.4 oz)* propane cylinders, *(enough to run the lantern and stove for one month)*, all for under one hundred dollars. For an additional one hundred and fifty dollars, she was able to put away enough food for one month. She also purchased 5 new, 5 gallon water jugs *(filled)* for under fifty dollars and a simple portable loo for about twenty five dollars.

Although on a tight budget, she has, for about three hundred dollars, provided everything she needs to ride out any storm for a month in comfort. *She says the peace of mind is worth a million dollars!*

In her storage cupboard she has put away enough food for 3 full meals a day, *(with lots of variety to prevent feelings of deprivation or depression)*, she has some comfort food for morale, and she is able to make her own skillet biscuits or breads. This is what she chose to store: *1 lg box of tea, 1 lg jar of coffee, 30 packaged drinks (tetra paks), 1 can hot chocolate mix, 1 box dry skim milk, 3 boxes granola and/or fruit bars, 2 boxes instant oatmeal packages, 1 lg jar peanut butter, 1 jar honey, 1 lg box each saltines, cheese crackers, melba toast, 2 packages instant cup-of-soup, 8 packages ramen-type noodles, 4 tins luncheon meat (ham, beef, chicken, turkey), 4 chili con carne, 6 cans pasta, 8 cans beans and sauce, 4 cans chili, 4 cans stews, 8 chunky soups, 2 cans each ham, chicken, salmon and tuna, 1 box instant potatoes, 1 lg bag converted rice, 4 cans each corn, peas, mixed veg, 2 packages each of lunchbox puddings, fruit cups and apple sauce, 2 bags of her favorite cookies, 10 handi-snak packages, 1 bag each raisins, dried fruits and chocolate chips, 1 bag of hard candy, 1-10 lb bag of all-purpose flour, 1-10 lb bag of multigrain flour, 1-10 lb bag of sugar, 1 box of salt, 1 can baking powder and 1 box soda, 2 cans shortening (plain and butter flavor), 1 bottle each olive and canola oils, 15 pkgs. of yeast and a vitamin/mineral supplement.*

Keeping Your Survival Cupboard *Safe*

Protecting Your Investment.

There are several factors that could adversely affect the *shelf-life* of food in your survival cupboard. Some are simple mistakes like storing fragrant dryer sheets or cleaning supplies near dry or packaged foods, or a more serious mistake, like storing your foods in a bad location or in the wrong containers. Unfortunately, *just one mistake* may seriously jeopardize what you have stored and could have life-threatening consequences.

The Storage Area.

In your home, designate an area for food and water storage and another area for nonfood items. This could be a seldom used bedroom, a closet or a new room built in the basement. Storage units or cupboards can be purchased or made at a reasonable cost to maximize the space you have available and keep things organized. For more space, add an extra shelf above the top shelf in closets or put shelves across the unused area under the basement stairs.

In an apartment, store food items in the *coolest* closets you have or designate an area of the bedroom, *(generally the coolest room)* to storage. If you have en-suite storage, convert part of it to shelves and store your food and water there. Store infrequently used closet items under the bed and use part of the closet for food storage.

Secrets to Successful Storage.

Keep it cool: The single most important factor necessary for foods to maintain their quality and nutritional value is a constant, cool temperature. ***The lower the temperature, the longer the shelf-life.*** Items stored at 40°F may last up to 5 years; at 70°F, 1-2 years; at 90°F, 6 months or less. Keep your storage area away from any appliances that give off heat, *(furnace, water heater, freezer or dryer)*, as they can cause temperature fluctuations which can cause foods to rapidly deteriorate. Also, ensure that the temperature doesn't dip below freezing in your storage area or you will lose most of your canned and jarred food items.

Keep it dry: High humidity is the worst enemy of dried and packaged foods as it accelerates the growth of bacteria and molds, promotes insect infestations and causes mustiness. A humidity level of 60% is best for dry food storage, but between 60-70% is still safe. Use a *humidity gauge* to determine the humidity level in your storage area. (*Note: A root cellar with fresh foods however, requires a higher humidity level*).

Keep your storage area dark: Light, whether sunlight or from an electric bulb produces physical and chemical changes in food, especially vitamin and mineral losses.

Choose the proper containers: Store foods in airtight, moisture-proof glass, metal or food grade plastic containers. The product label should tell you if the container is approved for food. If it doesn't say safe for food, don't buy it, or ask the store manager to check with the manufacturer. Don't use non-food grade plastic containers to store food, or those that have held anything other than food, as chemicals hazardous to your health may be transferred to your food. Using several smaller containers is better than one large container, because if something does spoil, your entire supply isn't ruined. Don't use plastic garbage cans to store loose, dry food or drinking water, as they are non-food grade plastic and may leach chemicals into the food or water.

Avoid chemical contamination: Always store non-food items away from food. Items such as fragrant dryer sheets, detergents, cleaning supplies, pesticides, kerosene and other non-food products release chemical vapors that are absorbed by dry and packaged foods, and can create a potentially serious hazard to your health.

The Enemies of Food.

Natural deterioration: Whether plant or animal, every living thing naturally deteriorates. An apple for example, contains enzymes which eventually cause the apple to discolor, become soft and spoil. Keeping foods cool is the best way to slow or retard this deterioration process. *Caution: if any item in your food storage cupboard shows signs of decay, remove it immediately before it causes other food to spoil.*

Microorganisms: The most common causes of food spoilage and food-borne illnesses, are bacteria, yeasts and molds. Again, storing your foods in smaller containers can stop the contamination from spreading throughout. Surface molds can be eliminated by wiping with a solution of 3 Tbl bleach in 1 quart of water. Molds on grains and legumes are serious, as they contain mycotoxins dangerous to both humans and animals. To be safe, dispose of anything you find with mold. To prevent mold, store grains, flour, beans, peanuts, etc., in airtight containers in a cool, dry place.

Insects and rodents: Packing your dry and packaged foods in airtight containers will prevent most insect infestations. Also, keeping the storage area clean will prevent rodents from being drawn to the area. Stuff steel wool in any hole that offers access to rodents.

Deadly cans and jars: Never use food from a can that is leaking, bulging, badly dented or has a bad smell. Toss food from jars that are cracked, or have loose or bulging lids. Never taste food from any container that *spurts* liquid when you open it.

Exotic Storage Treatments.

In general, the use of *nitrogen, dry ice, carbon dioxide, oxygen absorbers, desiccants and diatomacceous earth* to preserve food are not practical for the average home or apartment dweller. If these methods are of interest to you, ask the advice of a food storage professional.

Preventing Food Poisoning

Y2k and Food Poisoning.

Even with having all our modern amenities intact, food poisoning affects multi-millions of Americans each year. This is happening at a time when we can skip on down to the supermarket and choose from an incredible array of canned produce, fresh vegetables or meat butchered fresh each day. Our food is in the field one day and neatly wrapped on the shelves the next. Every step in the process features refrigeration and sanitation, and yet every single day, someone somewhere gets poisoned from their food. *What will happen as a result of Y2k disruptions?*

Everything, of course, hinges on how bad the Y2k disruptions are. If the electricity goes off, so does the refrigeration, the water supply and sanitation facilities. Possible fuel shortages and scheduling problems can bring a quick end to deliveries of our fresh meats and produce, and the resulting food shortages will force people to eat food that has been stored too long or stored improperly. Combine all this with a lack of proper sanitation and the possibilities of food poisoning will skyrocket.

What is Food Poisoning?

The term *food poisoning* normally describes an illness that originates from ingesting food or drink that is contaminated by bacteria or viruses. Anybody can be affected by food poisoning, but those most susceptible are seniors *(over 65)* and the very young *(under 4 years of age)*. Pregnant women and those already challenged by disease are also vulnerable.

The bacteria and viruses that cause food poisoning are normally part of our every day environment. Depending on the type of bacterial or viral contamination, our bodies can usually handle small amounts with no threat to our health, but once *they* are allowed to multiply we are at risk.

To multiply, bacteria need food, moisture and warm temperatures. The ideal temperature for bacterial growth is between 40°- 140°F. Above 140°F, heat *begins* to kill both bacteria and viruses. Above 160°F, death rates of both increase, with none living beyond 212°F. On the other side of the scale, below 40°F, growth of the bacteria slows. Once the food is frozen, growth stops, but the bacteria ***is not*** killed.

Therefore, the *number one* cause of food poisoning is keeping food too long at temperatures that support bacterial growth. In most instances, you can prevent food poisoning by observing the following simple rules:

- keep food clean
- cook food thoroughly
- keep hot food hot
- keep cold food cold

Keep Food Clean.

Sanitation may be a big problem during Y2k disruptions, so extra care will be needed. If the water is off, you will have to use stored water or scrounged water to clean counter tops, dishes or utensils. Be sure to properly treat any *scrounged* water before using. Boil it for a full three minutes and add a little bleach to act as a disinfectant.

Be especially careful with personal sanitation; wash your hands after going to the washroom and before touching any food. Don't allow anyone who is ill to handle, prepare or serve food. To avoid cross-contamination, wash your hands after touching any raw meats, poultry, seafood or eggs, before touching any other foods.

Cook Food Thoroughly.

Make sure that your meals are cooked at temperatures higher than 160°F, to kill bacteria. This is especially important in the case of raw meats such as, poultry, beef, pork and wild game. *Rare* beef is usually only cooked to 140°F and therefore some of the food poisoning bacteria may survive. Recent deaths occuring from E-*coli* were attributed to eating not fully cooked ground beef.

Keep Foods Hot or Cold.

Basically, avoid holding food at temperatures between 40°- 140°F for long periods of time, because this is the bacteria growth zone. To be safe, keep hot food above 140°F, and cold food below 40°F.

Symptoms of Food Poisoning.

Symptoms vary widely depending on the germ or toxin, but often people think they have the flu. The most common symptoms are: vomiting, diarrhea, headache and abdominal pains or cramps. Often there is a high fever including chills and sweats.

Avoiding Food Poisoning.

- Avoid day-old leftover meals by cooking only what you need for each meal.
- If you do have leftovers, reheat them ***only once*** and make sure the temperature reaches 160°F.
- Commercially canned foods are generally safe to eat right out of the can, but avoid any cans with bulging ends, spurting fluids, off-odor, mold, leakage or visible damage *(dented tin)*.
- Cook all meats until juices from the inside run clear, not pinkish. Take special care with ground meats as the grinding process itself mixes bacteria throughout.
- Cooked foods containing meat, fish, poultry, eggs and milk should never be allowed to sit at room temperature for longer than 2 hours.
- Never give babies ***unpasteurized*** honey as they can get botulism.
- Don't allow raw meats or fish to touch other foods such as salads or fruit, which will not be cooked before being eaten.
- Frozen foods which have been thawed should never be refrozen unless cooked thoroughly before re-freezing.

The Kitchen Gardener — Sprouting

Small, but Mighty.

Without any doubt, sprouting is the easiest, most inexpensive and most efficient way to provide an ***on-going supply*** of fresh, live, tasty food for your table. If, as feared and expected, Y2k glitches do cause extensive and lengthy food shortages, and the grocery stores are empty because of no deliveries, sprouting can easily save your life and the lives of your family. In fact, if you had nothing but sprouts to eat, you could live for the rest of your natural life, and enjoy better health and higher energy levels than you do now!

Sprouts, when eaten raw, are rich in vitamins, minerals, trace elements, live enzymes and fiber. Cooking them over 118°F, kills most of the live enzymes, but still leaves enough nutritional value for healthy living.

Your Sprouting Needs.

Aside from *untreated* seeds, water and temperatures above 50°F, all you need for successful sprouting are: a few wide-mouthed, quart-sized mason jars and a little bit of muslin, or some old nylon stockings to stretch over the mouth of the jar. Secure with elastic bands or string. You can also use nylon tulle from a fabric shop or *fiberglass* window screening.

Make sure that the seeds you buy for sprouting are untreated. Seeds for planting in gardens are likely treated with poisonous chemicals which can make them poisonous as sprouts. Seeds sold specifically for sprouting are your best bet, and can be obtained from companies specializing in sprouting seeds. Most health food stores carry seed varieties that can be sprouted, but the germination rates — although adequate — are less than those of specialty seeds. Also, be sure to get organically grown seeds to avoid possible chemical residues.

The most commonly sprouted seeds are mung beans, soybean and alfalfa, but many others are used, including wheat, corn, barley, clover, radish, French onion, green pea and sunflower. Avoid tomato and potato sprouts, as they are poisonous. Also, stay away from the sprouts of many ornamental flowers, foliage plants like hedges and shrubs, lawn seed and wild plants. Use only known sprouting seeds or ask the experts before trying anything exotic.

Sprouting Procedure.

1 Begin by soaking 1 to 4 tablespoons of seeds overnight in a wide-mouthed jar. Soak in 1 cup of water. Cover with fine mesh or cloth and secure with a rubber band or string.
2 Twice a day, swirl the seeds and a cup of fresh water in the jar

and invert to drain. Prop the jar at a 45° angle in a bowl to allow excess moisture to drain from the sprouts. When sprouting, don't use water that you cannot safely drink, as the water is taken into the sprouts.

3 The sprouts will be ready to use in about 3 to 6 days or when the sprouts are ½" to 1½" long. They can be eaten raw for maximum nutrition or cooked in soups, stews, stir-fries, bread, pancakes or just about anything else.
4 Cover the jar with plastic wrap and a rubber band, or transfer to a covered container, and store at about 35°- 40° F. They will keep for about 4 to 6 days if stored properly. Rinse sprouts well before chilling.

Sprouts grow in almost anything. If you don't have mason jars, use a glass bowl or a drinking glass. Once the seeds have soaked overnight, just rinse, drain and cover with a damp towel. The main thing is to lay in a couple of pounds of seeds so you can take advantage of sprouts as a food source.

Troubleshooting.

If your seeds sprout poorly, you may have old seeds, the temperature may be too cold or too hot, the seeds may not have been soaked long enough, or they may be too crowded in the jar. Also, make sure that your seeds are getting enough air circulation.

If they show signs of rot or mold, there may be too much water left in the container after rinsing, the temperature may be too hot, you may not be rinsing well enough, the sprouts could be too crowded in the container or you are not removing seeds that fail to sprout.

If you do see a bit of mold or rot, pick it out along with some of the surrounding healthy sprouts and discard. Don't confuse the fuzzy, white root hairs on some sprouts for mold.

If your sprouts are dry and withered, you may be exposing them to too much light, growing them in too hot an area or not giving them enough water.

Uses for Sprouts.

Use your imagination to come up with uses for sprouts, as they can be used in almost anything. Use them instead of shredded lettuce in tacos and pita pockets. Sprinkle some in your next grilled cheese sandwich or even in a peanut butter sandwich. Use sprouts in omelettes or corned beef hash. Add a half cup of sprouts when making a loaf of bread *(add with the liquids)*. Don't forget soups.

For some, sprouts are an acquired taste, but get used to eating them raw as a snack for maximum value. They are sure to be a most valuable addition to your survival cupboard. *Last tip:* alfalfa sprouts are the easiest to grow and are among the tastiest.

Small Space Gardening

Victory Gardens.

During the Second World War, food shortages and rationing were a part of daily life for those manning the homefront. As a result, citizens were encouraged to plant small gardens wherever possible; boulevards were torn up and planted, as were vacant city lots, back yards, balconies, and patios. These gardens were called Victory gardens. Any place that could grow food was put to good use. Y2k will force us to do likewise, as it brings transportation to a halt and prevents delivery of the fresh fruits and vegetables we have so come to depend upon!

Those of us in northern climes are used to going to the supermarket and choosing from an impressive array of vegetables and fruits from all over the world, but how do those fresh fruits and vegetables get here? Are they not shipped daily from where they are grown? Do they not come by boat, railway, truck or by air transport? And are all modes of transportation not likely to suffer major disruptions, if not complete breakdown, because of Y2k related problems?

At this present time, no railway, airline, or shipping company in the world is Y2k compliant! Lloyds of London — the famous worldwide insurance company — has already warned shipping lines that they will not insure ships that are not certified compliant, and so, it seems likely that few ships will be sailing. We can be almost certain that both the railways and airlines will be in complete chaos, leaving the trucking industry as our only semi-reliable form of transportation. But, will they be able to take the massive load? Will they have the fuel necessary? Will they be able to refuel as they cross the country? How will we get the food from Argentina, Asia, Brazil or Australia to the truckers?

Food Storage is the Best Solution!

There is little doubt that storing food is our *number one*, best and safest solution; so we should all commit to storing at least a six month supply of *canned* food. It is, however, entirely likely that our food supply could be disrupted for years! We must, therefore, become self-reliant by growing our own fresh vegetables, and this brings us to small space gardening.

Small Space Gardening.

If you own your own home and have a backyard, you will truly appreciate the fresh vegetables that a garden will provide for you and your family. Outdoor gardening, however, is a seasonal thing and those of us in the North during winter won't be able to grow anything outdoors except icicles! We will do well, though, if we *prepare* to grow whatever we can, *when* weather permits.

However, we might be able to grow some vegetables indoors, *if* we are able to keep our homes warm enough to prevent the plants from freezing.

If you are in the South when Y2k descends, you should be growing all that you can and preserving it for when your winter comes upon you. This is the perfect time for all of us to take up the *almost lost* art of home food canning

Again though, for those of us in the North, we believe that food storage is the *best* answer, but we also believe that every one of us should seriously plan on growing our own vegetables as soon as the weather permits. That means preparing ***NOW***, as shortages are also certain to be felt in every kind of garden supply. Stock up on your seeds, soils, containers, fertilizers, pest control, and vermiculite ***now***, while supplies are still available. If your local garden supply doesn't have any seeds presently in stock, try to purchase through some of the mail order suppliers.

In this book we will briefly deal with both small space, outdoor gardening and indoor container gardening. Both methods will prove to be extremely valuable over the next few years.

Small Garden — Big Results.
The most productive small space garden utilizes a combination of the French intensive gardening method and organic composting to provide the much needed natural fertilizer. When using this method, plants are spaced so closely that their leaves touch. This shades the soil and keeps it moist and warm. This type of garden is typically quite small *(i.e. 5′ x 5′ or 5′ x 10′)* and is designed to be tended from the sides to avoid walking in the garden itself. However, stepping stones can be placed to provide access to the more difficult-to-reach spots.

By using succession cropping *(as soon as one crop is out of the ground, the soil is quickly prepared and another vegetable is planted)*, two or even three crops can be taken out of the garden in one season. You can also produce more by starting your seeds elsewhere and transplanting the young plants into the garden. Each time a crop is replaced, the soil is refreshed with additional organic material.

Soil Preparation.
We are strongly recommending that everyone start their garden in the summer of 1999 to avoid food shortages in the year 2000. By starting before the year 2000, you should be able to *conveniently* have the soil well prepared. Bring in some well-rotted manure to enrich the soil and have someone with a rototiller mix it up for you. Work the manure or your compost into the soil until the top 12 inches are fully one-third to one-half organic matter. In clay-type soils, mix in one-third sand to provide better drainage and soil aeration.

Place your garden against a fence or build a wood or pipe frame about six feet high with vertical strings spaced about 6″ apart for the plants to climb on.

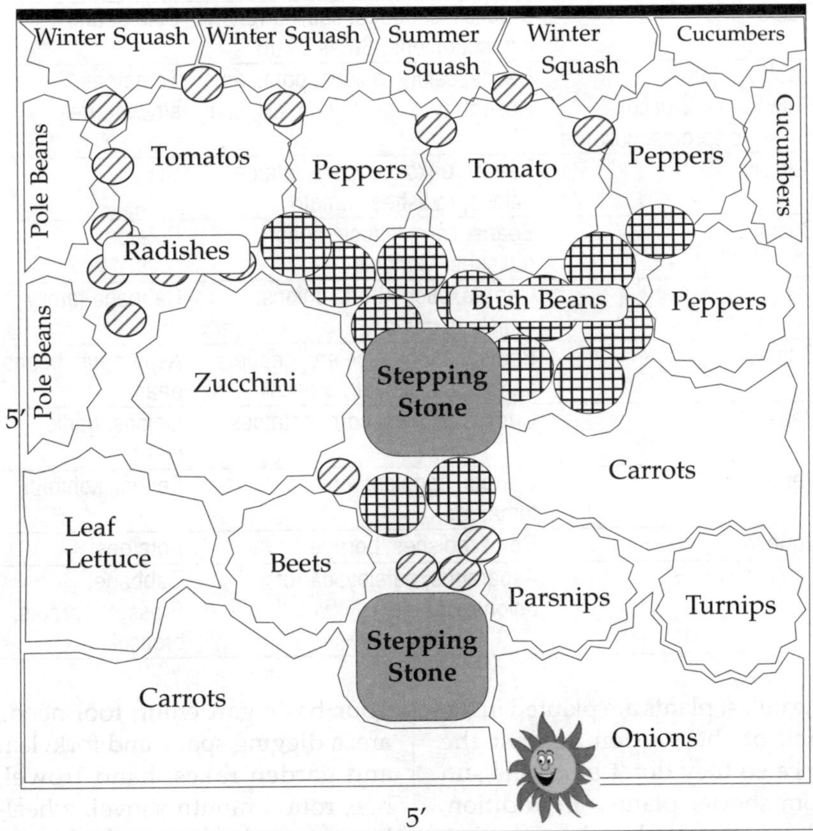

Adding these organic materials will increase the volume of your soil so that it forms a low mound, which aids drainage. Rake the mound smooth; then top it with a 2-inch layer of manure plus a bit of bone meal.

Position your garden where it will get the most sunshine throughout the day, but remember that the sun's travel path differs through spring, summer and fall. The amount of sun your garden gets will largely determine what you can grow. If you can get six or more hours of sunshine each day, you're in business. Under four and you had best buy canned vegetables or consider taking up sprouting to provide fresh, live greens.

The above diagram gives a rough idea of what your garden may look like, how intensively it can be planted and what plants companion well with others .

Vegetable	Plant with	Never plant near
Beans	Corn, cucumbers, eggplant, potatoes, radishes	Onions, leeks, kohlrabi, garlic
Beets	Broccoli, cabbage, cauliflower, lettuce, onions, Swiss chard	Pole beans
Cabbage family: Cauliflower, broccoli, Brussels sprouts, collards	Beans, celery, onions, potatoes, Rosemary, sage, thyme, dill, mint	Tomatoes, strawberries
Carrots	Beans, leeks, peppers, lettuce, onions, radishes, tomato	Dill
Cucumbers	Beans, corn, lettuce, peas, radishes, Marigold	Potatoes
Lettuce	Carrots, cucumbers, onions, radishes, garlic	Cabbage family
Onions	Beets, cabbage, celery, peppers, carrots, cauliflower, broccoli	Asparagus, beans, peas
Peas	Carrots, turnips, corn, potatoes	Onions, garlic, leeks
Peppers	Carrots, eggplant, onions, tomatoes	Fennel, kohlrabi
Squash	Corn, radishes, borage	Potatoes
Tomatoes	Asparagus, parsley, carrots, onions, borage	Cabbage, Brussels sprouts, broccoli

The tallest plants are planted in the back of the garden against the fence so they don't block the sun from shorter plants. In addition, all plants are placed near other plants which are known to grow well together *(companion planting). See the above chart.*

Start right away with your garden. Get some gardening books from the library and start planning. Order catalogues from some of the many seed companies out there, as they are loaded with good information about gardening. Above all else, start buying your seeds as soon as possible, for without them, you can't have any garden.

Your basic gardening tool needs are: a digging spade and fork, leaf and garden rakes, hand trowel, hoe, round-mouth shovel, wheelbarrow, garden hose and adapters and a watering can *(sprinkling can)*. If, as expected, the power grid is down, you won't have the luxury of water from the hose, so bear in mind that you may have to hand carry all your gardening water needs. You will then want a few tight sealing 3 or 5 gallon water containers and a wagon or two-wheel dolly to transport them to and from the nearest water source. This is also one of the main reasons for a small, but highly productive garden.

You will also want to have a few large containers to catch and store rain water. In fact, under survival conditions, you will want to rush quite a few containers outside when it rains.

Container Gardening.

Just about any vegetable that can be grown in a garden, can be grown in a container. Container sizes vary from huge ones which require their own wheels to move them about to the smaller, easy-to-carry sizes. Whatever sizes you choose to work with, all must be deep enough for the plants chosen and must allow water to drain from the bottom. Drainage holes are best if placed immediately above the bottom rather than in it. Place saucers or trays under the containers to avoid staining floors, furniture or windowsills. Empty the saucers after each watering.

Don't use soil from your garden in your containers, as it compacts too easily in containers, dries rapidly and drains poorly. You will obtain the best results by either using a professional planter mix or by making a homemade mix consisting of 2 gallons of garden soil with 2 gallons pearlite, 2 gallons of shredded peat moss, 2 tablespoons lime and 6-8 teaspoons of 5-10-10 fertilizer. Mix thoroughly.

One of the distinct advantages of containers is that the containers can be easily moved. This makes it possible to start plants indoors and move them outdoors during the day, or to shift plants throughout the day so they can get a bit more sunshine. Containers can be placed out in the yard, on a patio, a balcony, in a window or on a rooftop.

Before planting, soak unglazed clay pots in water first so they don't wick moisture from the soil. If re-using containers, scrub them out with a brush and a vinegar/water solution to remove any scaly deposits. Rinse with a mild bleach and water solution to prevent mold and disease problems. Rinse well with fresh, clean water.

Windowsill Farming.

Shelves can be built on the inside of windows to hold pots containing low-growing vegetables, such as: lettuce, spinach, carrots, beets, radishes, and dwarf tomatoes.

Plants grown indoors have the same needs for light and warmth as those grown outdoors. Any window with a southern or western exposure can be used to grow most vegetables. An east-facing window limits us to leafy vegetables and radishes. If you live in the Northern hemisphere, a north-facing window doesn't provide enough light to grow anything. *If you live in the Southern hemisphere, just replace every instance of north with south. The east and west remain the same.*

Plants grown in containers need watering more frequently than those in the garden — as much as

Plant Type	Shade Tolerance	Seeds or Transplant	Seed Depth	Minimum Container Size	Minimum Container Soil-depth
Beans green	Poor	S	1" deep	2 gallon	8" deep
Beets	Slight	S	¼" deep	½ quart	8-12" deep
Broccoli	Slight	T	¼" deep	5 gallon	18-20" deep
Brussel sprouts	Poor	S or T	¼" deep	5 gallon	18-20" deep
Cabbage	Slight	T	¼" deep	5 gallon	12" deep
Carrots	Slight	S	¼" deep	½ quart	8" deep
Cauliflower	Poor	T	¼" deep	5 gallon	18-20" deep
Collards	Slight	S	¼" deep	1 gallon	8-10" deep
Cucumbers	Slight	S	1" deep	5 gallon	18-20" deep
Eggplant	Poor	T	¼" deep	5 gallon	12" deep
Garlic	Slight	Clove	1" deep	1 gallon	6" deep
Lettuce	Good	S or T	¼" deep	½ gallon	8" deep
Onions	Good	S or T	¼" deep	½ gallon	8" deep
Peas	Good	S	1½" deep	1 quart	12" deep
Peppers	Poor	T	¼" deep	2 gallon	12" deep
Radishes	Slight	S	½" deep	½ quart	6-12" deep
Spinach	Good	S or T	½" deep	½ quart	8-10" deep
Squash	Poor	S or T	1" deep	5 gallon	24" deep
Swiss chard	Good	S or T	½" deep	3½ gallon	10-18" deep
Tomatoes	Poor	T	¼" deep	5 gallon	24" deep
Turnip	Slight	S	½" deep	5 gallon	12" deep
Zucchini	Poor	S or T	½" deep	5 gallon	18-24" deep

once each day in hot, dry weather. Test the top few inches of the soil with your finger to see how dry it is, or use one of the inexpensive moisture meters. If the soil feels dry, or reads dry, add water until it runs out the bottom drain holes. Then empty the saucer or catch tray underneath.

Handy Gardening Information.
The chart across the top of this page and the next page gives much information on most of the more common and more productive vegetables — use it when planning and planting your garden.

The type of plant you can grow in your garden is usually determined by the amount of sun you have available. If sunshine is limited, however, you can still grow a very useful garden by restricting yourself to the more shade-tolerant varieties. Varieties such as lettuce or Swiss chard.

Use the frost-tolerance column to avoid plant losses and time delays caused by planting too soon and being caught by the last spring frost. Or avoid even bigger losses caused by being caught by the first fall frost.

Plants per pot	Planting to Maturity	Min. / Optimum Germination Temperature	Frost Tolerance	Warm / Cool Season crop
4 plants	45-90 days	60/80 F°	None	Warm
2-3 plants	50-70 days	40/80 F°	Good	Cool
1 plant	60-90 days	40/80 F°	Very good	Cool
1 plant	70-130 days	40/80 F°	Very good	Cool
1 plant	65-110 days	40/80 F°	Good	Cool
3-4 plants	65-80 days	40/80 F°	Good	Cool
1 plant	65-70 days	40/80 F°	Some	Cool
2 plants	70-80 days	40/80 F°	Very good	Cool
1 plant	75-85 days	60/90 F°	None	Warm
1 plant	65-80 days	65/85 F°	None	Warm
3 plants	90-120 days	50/70 F°	Good	Cool
1 plant	40-80 days	40/70 F°	Some	Cool
3 plants	25-70 days	40/80 F°	Good	Cool
1 plant	55-70 days	40/70 F°	Some	Cool
1 plant	60-80 days	60/80 F°	None	Warm
4-6 plants	20-50 days	40/80 F°	Good	Cool
1 plant	40-50 days	40/70 F°	Good	Cool
1 plant	50-60 days	60/90 F°	None	Warm
4-5 plants	30-60 days	40/80 F°	Good	Cool
1 plant	55-90 days	50/80 F°	None	Warm
10-12 plants	35-60 days	40/80 F°	Very good	Cool
1 plant	65-110 days	60/90 F°	None	Warm

If planting a container garden, start your plants indoors from seeds or with starter plants from a garden supply center. Plants are normally started indoors and then hardened by gradually introducing them to the cooler outdoor temperatures. Once the plants are accustomed to cooler outside temperatures, they are transplanted into the garden after the risk of frost has passed.

If Y2k leaves us without electricity in winter, most Northerners will struggle with keeping their homes warm enough. The minimum germination temperature of seeds will then become very important to us. A thermometer will also be handy.

Container Soil Volumes.

The following chart shows the soil volumes for the more common clay pot sizes:

Size of	Approximate
3 inch	1 Cup
4 inch	1 quart
6 inch	2½ quarts
8 inch	1 gallon
10 inch	2½ gallons
12 inch	3½ gallons
14 inch	6 gallons

Fertilizing Plants in Containers.

Every three weeks lightly fertilize your plants. If using commercial fertilizers, be extremely careful not to overfertilize, as overfertilizing can easily damage or kill plants grown in containers.

Fertilizing with *organic* compost is the safest way to fertilize plants. For plants that are already rooted in containers, use a method called *"top-dressing"* or *"side-dressing"* to get the organic compost to your plants. Gently dig the organic fertilizer into the soil around plants as they grow *(use a kitchen knife in small pots)*. Some of the older soil can be removed to accommodate the new material.

Making Your Own Compost.

Composting is a natural process through which organic material is converted into a soil-like product called humus. Quality humus has a fresh, clean, earthy smell.

The ordinary home is a ready source of organic materials for composting. **From the garden:** leaves *(chopped to speed their breakdown)*, grass clippings *(not wet)*, plants and weeds *(without ripe seeds)*, old potting soil, soft plant stems, and some brush or wood chips. **From the kitchen:** any fruit or vegetable scraps, crushed egg shells, tea bags, coffee grounds with filters and some shredded paper. **Don't use:** meat, fish and bones, plastics, metal, fats and oils, dairy products, pet waste or any meat or cheese sauces.

Home composting can be done in many different *"build your own"* composters or with a commercial unit. Since many municipalities make composters available to residents at a very reasonable price, be sure to check with City Hall.

Composting can readily be done in a galvanized metal, aluminum or plastic garbage can or just as a heap in the back yard. To make a garbage can composter, set out a base of bricks or concrete blocks to support the garbage can. Drill some ½" holes in both the bottom and sides of the can to provide drainage and aeration.

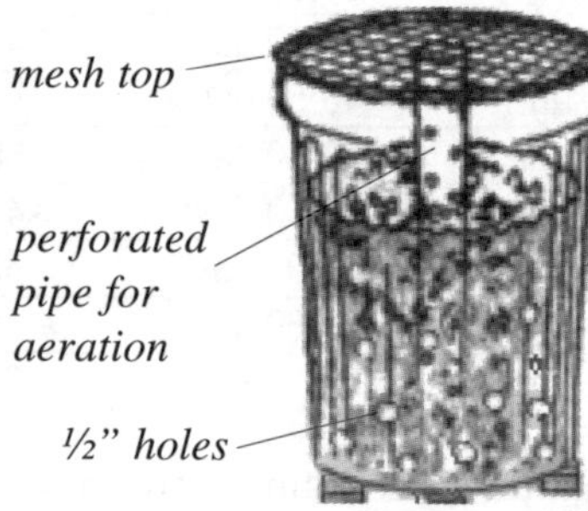

Cover the bottom with a small layer of fine branches to allow for good drainage and prevent the holes from blocking. Then alternate layers of wet *(e.g. kitchen scraps)* and dry *(e.g. yard material)* waste. Fill the entire can over time. Put a tray underneath if on a patio to prevent draining fluids from staining the patio.

Don't add thick layers of any one kind of waste. Grass layers should be no thicker than 2½"- 5" if mixed with dry, crushed leaves. To work well, composter contents should be moist like a wrung-out sponge. If the contents are too dry, it will take forever to compost; and if too wet, the contents will begin to smell.

If the composter is working well, the material will decrease in size and generate heat. Turn or mix the compost once a week or each time you add new material.

Troubleshooting Your Composter.

- If the center is damp and warm, but the rest is cold, the volume may be too small. Add more material to your composter.
- Bad odors? Turn and add some dry, crushed leaves. Loosen up the mass, break up clumps and add some fine branches or wood chips to help the pile *"breathe"*. Make sure that vent holes aren't blocked. A one inch layer of dirt on top will prevent bad odors.
- If compost doesn't decrease in size and generate heat, your composter needs some attention: if the pile is dry, add water and mix thoroughly; if it is wet and soggy, spread it in the sun and add dry material. Mix *"old"* compost with *"new"* material to speed action.
- If the pile smells sweet and is damp, but not heating — add grass clippings or table scraps.
- If compost attracts fruit flies, stir and add leaves or grass.
- Compost attracts wild animals? Always cover additions of food scraps with a layer of soil, or dig them into the mix. Keep a cover on your composter.

When to Start Composting?

Start your composting right away, as table scraps may be limited in the midst of Y2k disruptions. You can compost through the winter and be ready for spring gardening. The compost process slows down during the winter and will even stop completely when it freezes, but the freeze/thaw cycle actually helps the material to break down, and consequently decompose faster in the spring time when the action starts again.

How Long Does it Take?

The length of time needed to get finished compost depends on the design of your composter and the materials you use as compost. The size of the material used in your composter is also a factor — the finer it is, the faster the process. The composting process can take from two months to a year or more, depending on materials used and the composting method. To speed the process, try to maintain a good balance between wet and dry material, turn it frequently and make sure that waste is shredded into small pieces.

Put Compost to Good Use.

Compost is ready to use when it is dark in color, crumbles easily and has an earthy smell. It will benefit your garden by increasing the soil's moisture-holding capacity and its organic richness. Compost will provide your plants with much-needed nutrients, enhancing the growth of both root structure and edible product.

Insect and Pest Control.

Some insect damage is certain to happen to your garden or even to indoor plants in containers. Don't panic, but the sooner you act when you spot a bug, the sooner you can control the invasion.

One of the most effective methods of insect control is to simply pick them off by hand and dispose of the little critters. Squash them underfoot or with a stick or drop them in a container for disposal. Not all insects are harmful. Don't get rid of any green lacewings, ladybugs, or praying mantis'.

If possible, avoid the use of broad-spectrum pesticides in favor of the microbial method of pest control. Consult with your local garden center, *before the year 2000*, to find what microbial compounds work well on the pests that normally invade the plants that you intend to grow. Broad-spectrum pesticides kill all insects, including beneficial ones, whereas microbial products kill only harmful insects.

Some Basic Gardening Tips.

- If possible, place your garden where it will not be shaded by trees or buildings.
- Plant only vegetables that you and your family want to eat.
- Plant taller plants at the back of the garden so that all plants can benefit from the sun.
- Grow radishes among tomatoes and carrots as they will ripen and can be harvested before the tomatoes or carrots mature.
- When using the French intensive method, don't leave bare ground unplanted at any time during the growing season. This wastes space and allows the weeds to gain a foot-hold.
- Keep soil pH between 6.5 and 7.0 for most vegetables so that your plants can fully utilize all micronutrients from your soil. If you have problem soil, your garden supply center will send a sample of your soil away for analysis and advise you once the results are known.
- Plan on successive plantings of beans, lettuce and radishes to ensure a steady supply through the growing season. Always add more organic matter to the soil when replanting.
- Plant a few marigolds around the edges of your garden as they are proven to repel whiteflies, thrips, tomato hornworms, and root-knot nematodes.
- The best vegetables to grow are: tomatoes, green onions, leaf type lettuce, summer squash, zucchini, snow or snap peas, pole beans, beets, bush beans, carrots. *(The most valuable are listed first).*
- Don't plant your garden in rows, as the paths between rows are wasted space. It is much wiser and more productive to make two separate 5' x 5' gardens instead.
- Start your garden immediately. It will provide you and your family with an abundance of fresh food and help you through the upcoming difficult times.

The City Root Cellar

Your Cornucopia.

Fall harvest gives an abundance of vegetables and fruit just before winter. By using some well-proven root cellaring techniques, much of that abundance can be safely stored for use throughout the coming winter and spring and even into summer.

In this book, the term ***root cellaring*** encompasses vegetable-saving techniques that use non-electric cold storage methods. *Practical* methods of storage include the use of basement root cellars, stairwells, attics, balcony storage and leaving certain root crops in the garden, insulated by dirt and straw.

The Root Cellar.

The traditional root cellar had a dirt floor and was usually dug into the side of a hill or in the basement of a home. The dirt floor helped keep the temperatures low and constant, and the air moist, providing an almost perfect environment for long term storage of produce.

When placed in a basement, the root cellar should be built in the coldest corner. If your basement doesn't have a dirt floor you can increase moisture levels by keeping an open pan of water inside. Temperatures should be between 32°- 55°F, with a high humidity (*80-90%*). Check with a humidity gauge. Low to medium air circulation is best.

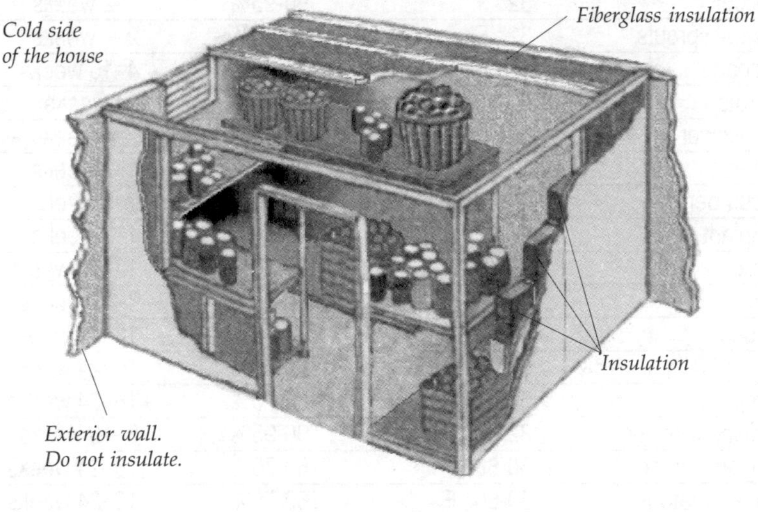

Built-in Basement Root Cellar

If possible, install a foundation vent in an existing window or through the concrete wall itself. The vent can be used to regulate the temperature in the room as outside temperatures vary with the season. Make sure you have both an accurate thermometer and a humidity gauge so that you are sure of the conditions in your root cellar. Combination units sell for under $25. Monitor them often.

The following table shows the type of produce that can be stored in a root cellar, the ideal conditions of storage and the resultant shelf-life. To get the maximum benefits from your root cellar, grow or buy those vegetables that keep the longest.

Stairwell Storage.

An *enclosed*, outside basement stairwell can be used to store root crops. Simply keep the produce in baskets along the sides of the stairs — the higher steps *(closer to the outdoors)* are the coldest. Install a door on the basement side and use the door to control temperatures in the stairwell — open to warm, close to cool.

In-Garden Storage.

One of the easiest ways to store some crops, such as: cabbage, celery, carrots, collards, kale and parsnips, is to leave them in the garden. Simply cover them with mulch *(leaves, straw or peat)*. Hold the mulch in place with boards or

Produce	Ideal Storage Temperature	Ideal Relative Humidity	Approximate Shelf-Life
Apples	32° F	90-95%	16–24 weeks
Beets	32-40° F	90-95%	12–20 weeks
Broccoli	32° F	90-95%	1–2 weeks
Brussel sprouts	32° F	90-95%	2–4 weeks
Cabbage	32° F	80-90%	4–16 weeks
Carrots	32-40° F	90-95%	24 weeks
Cauliflower	32° F	80-90%	2–4 weeks
Collards	32-40° F	90-95%	1–2 weeks
Cucumbers	40-50° F	85-90%	2–3 weeks
Eggplant	50-60° F	85-90%	1–2 weeks
Garlic	35-40° F	60-70%	12–16 weeks
Leeks	32° F	90-95%	4–12 weeks
Onions	35-40° F	60-70%	16–24 weeks
Potatoes	32-40° F	80-90%	16–24 weeks
Pumpkins	50-60° F	60-70%	16–24 weeks
Radishes, winter	32-40° F	90-95%	8–16 weeks
Squash, winter	50-60° F	60-70%	16–24 weeks
Sweet potatoes	50-60° F	60-70%	16–24 weeks
Tomatoes, green	55-65° F	85-90%	4–6 weeks
Turnip	32-40° F	90-95%	8–16 weeks

cover with some dirt. By using this method, some crops can be safely left in the ground from the end of one growing season until the beginning of the next. The hardware cloth between the plants and the mulch gives protection from mice and other unwanted guests. Rake the dirt into raised mounds on either side of the row before placing the hardware cloth and the mulch.

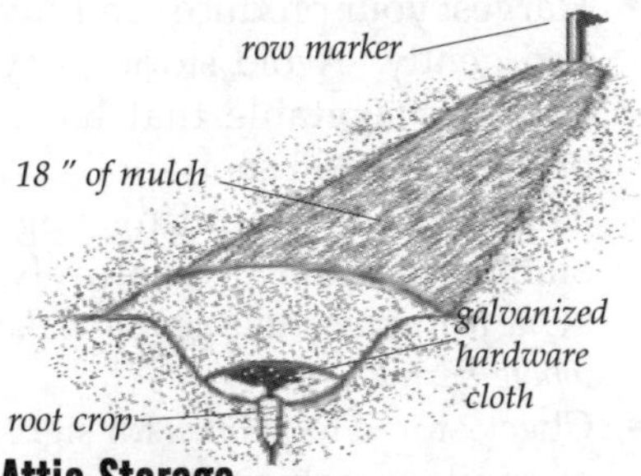

Attic Storage.

Root crops can be stored in unheated attics over the winter. If your attic doesn't have a wooden floor, cover rafters with planks to provide a safe place to put the containers and to walk. Store vegetables in either cardboard boxes lined with plastic or in small 18" high, plastic trash containers with clamp-on lids.

Place a layer of vegetables on a 3" layer of damp sand then alternate between more sand, vegetables, sand, and so on, until container is full. Most attics hold a relatively constant temperature between 35°-40°F in winter, but be careful to check the temperature on sunny days as it can warm quickly.

Balcony Storage.

Aside from buying and storing *canned* fruit and vegetables, the best advice we can give to the modern city apartment dweller is to buy a few styrofoam or double-walled, insulated coolers in which to store a few vegetables. These coolers can be stacked neatly in the corner of your balcony. Buy sand to layer the vegetables from any garden supply center.

This is most useful in areas where the outside winter temperatures stay steady between 32°- 55°F. In colder areas, carefully watch the temperatures and be prepared to move the containers to prevent produce from freezing.

Preparing Your Produce.

Beets: Harvest once nights drop to 30°F. Leave the root intact and about 1 inch of stem on top; if you cut too close to the beet, it will lose moisture, dry-out and spoil.

Cabbage: Remove loose outer leaves and wrap in newspaper. Store in a box. Since cabbage can give off quite an aroma, a better procedure might be to store your cabbage, root up, in damp sand in a garbage can.

Carrots: Harvest carrots before the ground freezes solid. Snap the stems off and lay carrots side by side on a one-inch layer of damp sawdust. Arrange one layer of carrots and then put another inch of damp sawdust followed by an-

other layer of carrots, etc.. Don't stack carrots on top of each other, but they can touch, side to side.
Celery: Don't remove the leaves or roots. Replant celery in boxes containing moist sand. Plant side by side until box is full.
Leeks: Replant side by side in moist sand in your root cellar.
Garlic: Keep cool in a paper bag.
Onions: Pull onions after the tops have fallen over in the row, turned yellow and started to dry. Cut off the tops, leaving a one inch stub, and dry them on screens under cover for two to three weeks. Turn them several times to dry. When dry, hang them in the root cellar in some old nylon stockings, as shown.

Parsnips: Can be left in the garden covered with mulch or even frozen in the ground and dug as needed, or harvested after the first frost and layered with sawdust or moist sand.
Potatoes: Dig after the vines have been dead for about 2 weeks. Keep them in moist air for about 2 weeks between 65-75°F to toughen the skins, but don't leave them in the sun or wind. Then store in covered boxes away from light to prevent them from sprouting or turning green (*greenish colored potato skins indicate the presence of poisonous alkaloids — dispose of any potatoes with greenish skins*).
Rutabagas: Cut off tops and leave roots intact. Layer in plastic-lined boxes with moist sand.
Winter Squash: Harvest just before the first frost and let them cure for about two weeks at 70°F so that the skins can toughen. Always leave a stub stem, as the soft scar on a stemless squash invites spoilage. Store in a dry place at 55°F.
Turnips: Leave a short stub of the tops and the root intact. Layer with moist sand.

Tips for Root Cellaring.

- Harvest your produce carefully and gently. Avoid storing any fruit or vegetable that has a bruise, as it will soon spoil and cause the surrounding vegetables to spoil prematurely. *"One bad apple really can spoil the whole barrel."*
- Check stored food *often* for signs of spoilage; remove any questionable produce immediately.
- Don't ever store insect damaged vegetables or fruit.
- Never place produce directly on the floor; store it in containers a few inches above the floor to allow for air circulation.
- Instead of building shelves of solid wood, use 1 x 3's spaced ½" apart to allow for better air circulation.
- If possible, chill produce before putting it in your root cellar, as the sudden introduction of large volumes of warm vegetables or fruits will raise the temperature of your root cellar and any previously stored produce.

Your Own On-Going Meat Supply

Small Investment — Big Returns.
If, as expected, Y2k leaves us with empty grocery store shelves, raising rabbits could be one of the best solutions. They are the perfect small animal for the backyard meat producer. They take little space; can be raised indoors or outdoors; their manure is easy to handle and is a good fertilizer for the garden; they reproduce quickly and are easy to butcher — once you get beyond the trauma of having to kill them. If you want to successfully raise rabbits, you must detach yourself from them emotionally. If, however, you or your children must have one as a pet, set one aside as the family pet and raise the others for food or trade.

Rabbits not only supply one of the leanest, highest-protein meats, but they are also one of the finest and most desired barter items to have on hand. Trade one or two for some fuel, flour or anything else you might be needing. Their meat will always be in high demand in a depressed marketplace.

Your family can have rabbit to eat at least once a week by keeping just two does and one buck. Each doe will have four to seven litters a year, each of about six young. Keeping ten does and one buck will provide you with about 300 rabbits a year, enough for all your needs and plenty of meat to sell or barter.

Getting Started.
Start by checking into your local zoning bylaws to ensure that your project is legal. If you decide to breed your rabbits indoors, you shouldn't have any problems with the bylaws, but you probably need to be legal if you have your hutches *visible* in the backyard.

Considering the problems that Y2k may cause, it might be wise to plan on breeding your rabbits indoors to protect your investment from theft — out of sight, out of mind! Start with two does and one buck. If desired, you can expand later. Be sure to purchase any new does from some other lineage to avoid inbreeding problems.

The undisputed leaders for meat production are the New Zealand Whites and the Californian. Both are medium-sized rabbits with rapid growth when young. Either breed will reach a weight of about 4 to 4½ lbs. in only eight to ten weeks. You can, therefore, harvest the meat without spending a lot of money on feed.

Buy your breeders from a reliable source, and be sure to take a look at their living conditions. Are they clean? Are the rabbits content and healthy? Are they well treated? Start with rabbits that are three to five months old, as *"proven breeders"* are often expensive or *"worn out"* before you get them.

Rabbit Hutches or Cages.

To prevent theft, we recommend raising your rabbits indoors. However, the healthiest rabbits are raised in outdoor hutches similar to the one pictured below.

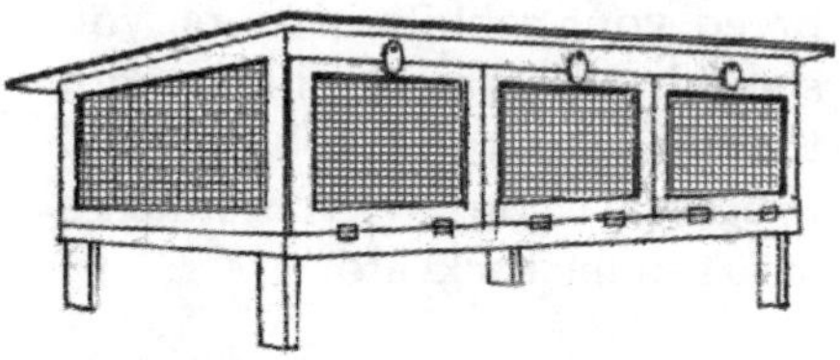

A hutch like this can be built out of scrap lumber, but the wire mesh will have to be purchased. There is a mesh specifically designed for rabbits. Rabbits love to chew wood so all sides, including the floor and ceiling should be covered with the mesh. The use of mesh on the floor of each cage allows waste to drop to a tray below. The roof can be plywood covered with shingles or roll roofing. The average size of each pen is 3′ x 2′ x 18″ high.

These hutches can be built two or three tiers high to accommodate more rabbits. Each pen must have its own waste collection tray and each pen holds only one rabbit. Plan enough pens to accommodate the litters from each doe. Place the hutch where it will be shaded from the heat of the sun in summer.

Keep the buck in the center pen and a doe on either side. The does can be mated once they are five months of age. To mate, take the doe from her pen and place her in with the buck, rump first. If both are ready, he will mount her and mating will take place within minutes. Watch the process and once mating has taken place, remove her and put her back in her own pen. If he doesn't mount her, bring her back in six hours for another five minutes. Record the date of mating and the name of the buck in a book. She will give birth *(kindle)* in 28 to 31 days.

Continue the normal rate of feed for the doe *(4 oz of pellets in 2 feedings per day)* until the twentieth day of her pregnancy, then double her rations to accommodate the rapid growth of the unborn babies. Make sure she has plenty of fresh water to drink. Actually, none of your rabbits should **ever** be without fresh water to drink.

Be sure to put a nest box in her cage a couple of days before she is due to give birth. Put a bit of soft straw and some wood shavings in the nest box. She will arrange it to suit herself. A nest box is pictured below. She will pluck fur from her neck and between her front legs to line the nest.

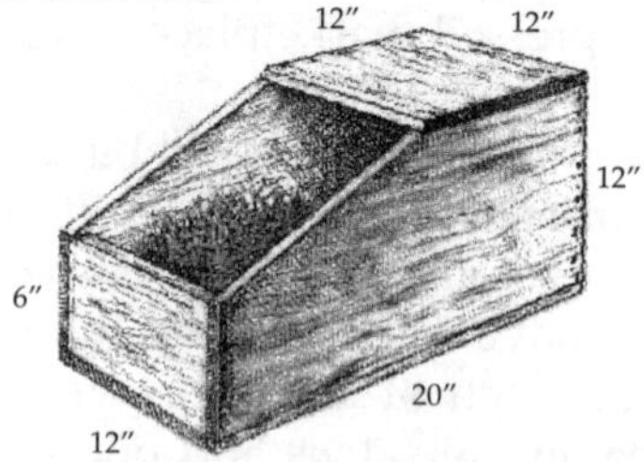

Maintain the high rate of feed for the doe until about three weeks after she has kindled. At ten days the young will open their eyes and in about three weeks they will be hopping around and eating some of her food. Young rabbits can be weaned from the mother after four weeks and placed in their own cage. In eight to ten weeks they can be butchered.

Cannibalism.

Sometimes the doe will get carried away with cleaning up the membrane after giving birth and may actually eat her young. This can be caused by a lack of water while giving birth or by the stress of a difficult birth. Don't dispose of her, simply try breeding again in about three weeks.

Housing Sanitation.

Sanitation is critically important for the health and well-being of your rabbits. It is also one of the main reasons for using wire mesh only floors in cages *(with catch tray placed below the mesh)*. Experienced breeders know that poor sanitation is an invitation for potentially disastrous diseases among rabbits, and are especially careful to keep hutches scrupulously clean.

The propane torch is considered the most reliable method of killing germs on cage wire and wooden parts of outdoor hutches. The torch flame kills germs and singes off unwanted hair. A brush easily removes ash residues. Disinfecting with liquids causes the hair to stick to the cage, making it almost impossible to remove. Nests used for kindling should be sanitized after every use.

Helpful Tips for Raising Rabbits.

- When breeding, never take the buck to the female, as she may defend her territory and can do serious damage to him!
- Most young bucks don't want to be bred more than once a week. Keep ten does maximum per buck.
- Put two meshes an inch apart between adjacent pens to keep rabbits from injuring each other through the mesh.
- Use all-wire cages for breeding indoors. Each should have a tray under the mesh floor to catch droppings. Don't keep your rabbits in an unlit area; they like to see daylight as much as you do.
- Apartment dwellers ***can*** raise rabbits indoors or on a balcony, but keep your operation clean to avoid complaints from your neighbors.
- Be very careful when examining newborn rabbits. Distract the mother by giving her some nice, fresh lettuce to nibble on. Rub some rabbit excreta on your hand before moving back the fur covering the babies. Count them and remove any dead, undersized or deformed young. Replace the fur.
- The best way to be certain that your rabbits are getting all the nutrition they need is to feed them on a commercial pelletized feed. You can supplement with cabbage or lettuce, but don't count on feeding greens only; your rabbits will starve to death.

Chickens.

Chickens can supply you with both meat and eggs, but unless you have a backyard available and are willing to build a proper chicken coop, plan on buying canned chicken and powdered eggs. This is not a practical project for the city apartment dweller, but it could be an excellent neighborhood project involving and feeding four or five families. Again though, be sure to check your local zoning bylaws before starting, but consider also that after Y2k, zoning bylaws may not mean very much to anyone — including the authorities!

One of the hallmarks of rural life is the willingness of neighbor to help neighbor. This is something that has been lost to most city dwellers over the years. In fact, most of us don't even know our neighbors even though we may have lived beside them for many, many years! Y2k may force us to make changes in how we relate to one another. Why not start now?

Get a number of families together and talk about Y2k. Once everyone understands the possible problems that Y2k could cause, and realizes that these problems are very likely to happen, they should be extremely receptive to a cooperative venture like this. Perhaps a neighbor with a large backyard would be happy to have a chicken coop and run built in their backyard. Everyone shares equally in the expenses, labor, meat and eggs.

Consult your library for books on how to house and raise chickens. Then, decide on how many and what type of chickens your group will purchase. Lastly, design the coop and decide how large the fenced-in chicken run will be. You might even be fortunate and find that some of your older neighbors already know exactly what to do.

Try to have everything in place and fully operative well before Y2k hits. For instance, by preplanning you can use electric heat lamps to brood day-old chicks — a luxury which may not be available to us for a number of months after January 1, 2000. By preparing early, you may avoid delivery problems and possible shortages in both building supplies and chickens.

A Few Tips on Chickens.

- Chickens are bred to produce either meat or eggs, but not both; the best egg layers normally don't have a lot of meat and those with meaty carcasses tend to lay few eggs.
- Breeds that provide a fair balance of both eggs and meat are: the *Rhode Island Reds* and the *White, Barred and Plymouth Rocks*. The *Rhode Island Reds* are excellent chickens to raise in colder climates, as they tolerate cold well.
- Mash purchased from a feed supply store is the most common food for chickens.
- Each chicken needs at least two cups of water daily, since eggs are almost entirely water.

Barter — The New Economy

When Times Get Tough.

In a normal economy, paper money and coins are the usual and most convenient medium of exchange. However, the economy *will not* be normal after Y2k! In fact, even now in 1998, the global economy shows numerous signs of strain and imminent collapse.

It is well beyond the scope of this book to discuss the financial woes of the world, but we fail to see how our already frail, chronically ailing economy can escape the disaster that is sure to be brought about by all the Y2k computer failures. When we read that countries such as Japan, China and Russia, as well as entire continents such as Asia, Europe and South America are hardly doing anything about Y2k, we find it hard to believe that the international banking system can survive.

It seems quite obvious that much more *mis-information* about Y2k compliance in government, industry and the world of finance exists, than does truth. Y2k failures can easily shut down all industry — causing unprecedented levels of unemployment — plus bring down the banking system and communications.

Do I hope that chaos will happen? Absolutely not! I hope and pray that we will all cruise through the year 2000 without difficulty, but cannot help but fear that in reality we will experience the worst. I would, therefore, rather prepare and survive, than to not prepare and find myself and my family helpless, cold and starving. If the worst does happen, at least we're prepared. If nothing happens, we can always give our stored food supplies to the food bank and bless someone else.

If the Banks Fail.

If Y2k does cause the banks and banking system to fail, we will be unable to get cash, unless we have some set aside. So, if you can, set as much cash (*paper money*) aside as you can afford. In addition, buy as much silver, gold and platinum as you can afford. Get either coins or the smallest possible ingots, so that you have small, measurable quantities to trade for needed goods or services. Barter, after all, is the art of trading something you have in abundance for something you lack and need.

For instance, you might trade one or two gold coins for a half a cow; or you might trade a rabbit for a chicken, or some eggs. You can trade just about anything for anything as long as you have someone who wants what you have. At the end of the Second World War, cigarettes were worth much more than money! If you had cigarettes, you had a lot of power. During the war, cooking oil was worth its weight in gold, literally — it allowed you to eat, whereas you couldn't eat gold!

When bartering, keep your eyes and ears open. It sometimes pays to know what others want and need. For instance, you might hear of someone who wants some .22 Long Rifle cartridges. In spite of the fact that you don't personally want any cartridges, you might trade something to someone else to get some cartridges to trade for something that you do want.

Barter Items.

So, what items are generally the best items for barter? Depending upon your personal beliefs, some of the most highly *sought-after* items may cause you to have a bit of a moral dilemma; for example, tobacco and liquor products. They are often considered immoral by some, because of their addictive and destructive nature, but are usually the most sought-after and measurable items. Cigarettes can be bought and stored by the carton and traded by the carton, the package, or broken down into 1, 2 or 5 cigarettes. Liquor comes in a wide variety of sizes. Both can demand high prices from those who feel they can't live without them.

Here are some other barterable items: any kind of stored food or water, coffee, tea, coffee filters, fuel for campstoves, propane, motor oil, kerosene, gasoline, spark plugs, cigarette lighters, matches, candles, wax, dish soap, laundry soap, bath soap, disposable razors, toothpaste, toothbrushes, toilet paper, women's sanitary napkins *(also make excellent wound dressings)*, medical tape, bandages, safety pins, bleach, paper, crayons, paints, pencils, notebooks, books, Bibles, nails, rope, string, etc..

Garden supplies, such as: seeds *(non-hybrid are the best)*, organic seeds and grains for sprouting, *sprouts*, potting soils, peat moss, composted waste, fertilizers, and even earthworms *(raise some good insects like the ladybug for organic pest control)*.

Clothing items, such as: shoes, socks, underwear, thermal socks, wool socks, sewing patterns, wool, fabric, knitted items, needles, thread, baby clothes, blankets, and cold-weather gear.

Canning supplies, such as: mason jars, sealing rings, vinegar, pickling spices, canning salt, paraffin wax for sealing, alum, cheesecloth, and, of course, any kind of fresh garden vegetable or fruit for canning.

Don't forget services. Maybe you can paint or build something for someone in trade for something you need. Everybody has a skill. What can you trade?

Lastly, don't trade from a position of weakness. Be prepared to walk away from a bad deal in search of a better one. Someone out there desperately wants what you have!

Index

A

Attic Storage 101

B

Baby food 52
Bacteria 27
Barbecue grills 21
Barter 103, 107
  Items 108
Beans 59
  Cooking of 60
  Storing of 59
  Varieties 61
Bleach 28
Bread 69
  Unyeasted 69, 72
  Yeasted 69, 70

C

Calcium hypochlorite 29
Campstoves 16
  Liquid fuel 16
  Propane 16
Campstove Cookin' 75
Candles 18
Carbon monoxide 15, 20
  Detector 15, 20
    Limitations 21
  Symptoms of poisoning 21
  Treatment 21
Cast-iron cookware 73
Chickens 106
Chlorine 28
Cholera 27, 40
Companion planting 92
Composting 96
  Materials 96
  Troubleshooting 97
Construction toilets 40
Cooking Supplies 41

D

Denial (*Y2k*) 6, 8
Dental needs 43
Diarrhea 27
Distillation 30

E

E.P.A. 26
Seniors 21
Electric generator 21
Electric outage 5, 13
  Expected duration 13, 24
Electricity 10
Embedded microprocessors 7
  Estimated number of 7
Equivalents 80

F

F.E.M.A. 29
Fertilizing plants 96
  Organic composting 96
  Top-dressing 96
Filter pump 28
Fire 15, 21, 22
  Prevention 22
  Procedures 22
  Types of fires 22
Fireplace 19
  Damper 20
  Efficiency 20
  Gas 19
Flashlight 18
Flour 68
  Storing of 69
  Varieties 73, 74
Fluorescent lamp 18
Food poisoning 85
  Causes 85
  Symptoms of 86
Food shortages 5, 87
Food Storage 49, 83, 89
  containers 83
Food Storage Mistakes 49
Frost-tolerance 94
Fuel
  Coleman fuel 15
  Iosol 15, 20
  Propane 15, 22
Fuel storage 13
  Fuel needs 14

G

General Motors 9
Gold 107
Grains 67
  Cooking of 67,68
  Storing of 67
  Varieties 68

H

Handy gardening information 94
Home heating 14
Hours of sunshine 91, 93

I

In-Garden Storage 100
Infants 21
Ingots 107

J

Just in time inventorying 9

K

Kerosene Lantern 18
Kitchen Equipment 41

L

Legacy systems 6

M

Mantle lamps 15
- Liquid fuel 16
- Propane 17

Memory joggers
- Adults 35
- Baby 33
- Kids 34
- Just-in-case 36
- Pets 37
- Seniors 36
- Special Needs 37
- Teens 34
- Toddlers 34

Microfilter pump 27, 32
Minimum germination temperature 95

N

N.E.R.C 11

P

Pasta 65
- Cooking of 65, 66
- Storing of 65
- Varieties 66

Pit Latrine 40
Porta-potty 40
Portable loo 40
Power grid failures 10
Programming
- Obsolete computer languages 7
- Time involved 7
- Yet to be done 6

Protozoa 27

R

Rabbits
- Breeding 104
- Hutches 104
- Raising 103

Railroad 12
Rationing 32
Recipes
- Breakfast 75
- Lunch 76
- Supper 76

Rice 62
- Cooking of 63
- Storing of 62
- Varieties 64

Riverbank infiltration 31
Rolling boil 32
Root Cellaring 99
- In Stairwell 100
- Preparing produce 101
- Shelf life 100
- Tips 102

S

SCADA 11
Self-reliance
- First aid 42
- Sewage disposal 40

Siphon 24, 25
Smoke detector 22
Soil preparation 90
Soil volumes 95
Sprouting 87, 91
Sterno fuel 19
Substitutions 79,80
Succession cropping 90

T

The Domino Effect 9
Treating stored water 26
Trench Latrine 40

U

US Social Security Administration 7

V

Victory Gardens 89
Viruses 27

W

Water 23
- Distillation 30
- Organisms in 27
- Riverbank infiltration 31
- Storage 23, 24
  - Containers 25
- Treating 26, 28, 29

Windowsill farming 93
Wood Burning 19

Y

Y2k 6
- What is Y2k? 6